THE HAMLYN GUIDE TO

COMMERCIAL
AIRCRAFT
&AIRLINE
MARKINGS

THE HAMLYN GUIDE TO

COMMERCIAL
AIRCRAFT
& AIRLINE
MARKINGS

CHRISTY CAMPBELL

HAMLYN

The publishers would like to thank Technical Editor Leo Marriott
for his assistance in the preparation of this book

First published in 1992
Hamlyn is an imprint of Octopus Illustrated Publishing
Michelin House, 81 Fulham Road, London SW3 6RB
part of Reed International Books Ltd

A catalogue record for this book is available from
the British Library.

ISBN 0 600 57450 4

Produced by Mandarin Offset

Printed and bound in Hong Kong

CONTENTS

Introduction

Swissair, Airbus Industrie A310

In the years since World War II the commercial air transport industry has changed the face of the world. Whereas travel was almost exclusively a pastime for the wealthy, there is now ample opportunity for the ordinary working person to fly away on holiday to far flung parts of the world that his parents perhaps only glimpsed in films, books or magazines. Of course it is not only for leisure that people travel. Today's business community is truly international with executives, salesmen, scientists, engineers and others regularly shuttling from one country to another in the course of their everyday work. The major cities of the world are becoming more and more cosmopolitan as people of all nationalities walk the streets, the shops sell goods from around the world and the restaurants serve fresh food flown from the world's diverse agricultures.

A visit to any of the world's major airports will reveal how these people and goods are moved around the globe so efficiently. A steady flow of airliners, seemingly ever increasing in size and capacity, arrives and departs throughout the 24 hours of the day almost unaffected by climate and weather. In the busier regions, the main factor which upsets the smooth flow is the congestion in the skies caused by the sheer proliferation of airlines and aircraft, a problem putting mounting pressure on the world wide Air Traffic Control network which is a vital part of the service infrastructure supporting aviation activities around the globe.

Although much pioneering of the world's air routes took place in the years between the two World Wars (1918-1939), the aircraft and equipment of the time were basic in nature. Aircraft were slow, taking days and even weeks to complete long distance flights. Passenger loads were small, limited by the size and performance of the aircraft, and timetables were often disrupted because of weather problems. Lack of navigation facilities and blind flying aids often led to crashes which endowed the fledgling air transport industry with a dramatic and risk laden image which did little to encourage mass trave!.

As is often the case, many of the advances in technology have come from the impetus of war and this is particularly true of civil aviation. During World War II there were tremendous strides in the development of jet engines, large multi-engined transport aircraft, radar, electronic navigation aids and many other techniques and equipment which were directly applicable to civil flying. The onset of the Cold War in the late 1940s led to the Berlin airlift of 1948 where a major city was supplied totally by air transport for almost a whole year. Although this was almost entirely a military operation, it was a dramatic demonstration of the capabilities of post-war aviation and many of the personalities involved went on to play major roles in the civil airline world.

In the 1950s the airliner market was dominated by America with famous aircraft such as the Douglas DC-4 and DC-6, the graceful Lockheed Constellation, the luxurious Boeing Stratocruiser (directly developed from the B29 Superfortress bomber) and the practical range of twin-engined Convairliners. In the meantime, Britain attempted to build on its lead in jet engine technology and flew the world's first jet airliner, the de Havilland Comet, in 1949. However, a series of disastrous crashes set this programme back by almost a decade by which time American industry had moved on to a new generation of airliners such as the Boeing 707 and DC-8. Of some consolation to the British was the success of the Vickers Viscount, the world's first successful turboprop airliner which sold widely on both sides of the Atlantic.

However it was the new American aircraft which set the pace and ushered in the dawn of the civil jet age around 1959. Since then, airliners have increased steadily in size, efficiency, range, and safety but there has been virtually no change in the speed of air transport. Most current jets cruise at around 450-500kts, exactly the same as the Boeing 707. The one glamourous exception is, of course, the beautiful Anglo-French Concorde which, for almost two decades, has been the only supersonic transport aircraft and has carved out an enviable niche in the market for its only operators, British Airways and Air France. In recent years this has not been the only European aircraft to challenge the established American manufacturers. The multi-national, French-based Airbus Industrie has slowly gained strength since its establishment in 1969 and today has a sophisticated range of airliners available to meet the needs of the world's airlines. Currently, it accounts for around one third of world sales in the medium and large categories of aircraft and has established a firm reputation in applying new technology to improve the safety and efficiency of its aircraft.

American industry has not been slow to respond and both McDonnell Douglas and Boeing have a comprehensive range of new aircraft available. McDonnell Douglas has traditionally gone for the evolutionary approach so that the DC-9 of the 1960s and 70s has become the basis for the MD-80 series and the new MD-90s, while the DC-10 has evolved into the MD-11, with the MD-12 in prospect. On the other hand, Boeing have often taken the innovative path, producing something entirely new to meet changing requirements. The classic example was the massive 747 which currently dominates the world's long haul airline fleets, and recently Boeing launched the all new 777.

Consideration of the large, long-range aircraft should not detract from the thousands of smaller aircraft, jet and turboprop powered, which make up the bulk of many of the world's airline fleets. There has been just as much progress here, and today many far flung towns and communities are provided with a first class modern service from their local airport by aircraft such as the BAe.146, the Fokker 100, ATR72, and Dash 8. The development of comfortable regional air services means that business and leisure travellers can often fly from their local airport directly to their intended destination, or to a major hub airport to continue their journey on a modern long haul jet. There are few parts of the world which today are not accessible by scheduled airline.

In this book the reader will be able to review some forty airliner types. Although all current large airliners are included, there must of necessity be others that have been excluded for reasons of space. These are mostly the older jets which are unlikely to remain in service much longer, such as the Caravelle (a world leader in its time), and smaller but numerous turboprop commuter airliners such as the Jetstream, Metro and Bandierante. As a general guide only those aircraft carrying 30 or more passengers have been considered eligible for inclusion.

The greater part of this book deals with the airlines themselves, for the aircraft are but the tools of the organizations that use them. An airline is a complex organization and in addition to the crews that fly the aircraft it needs engineers and maintenance crews to look after them, sales and marketing staff to provide the passengers, ticketing and reservation clerks to process customers, and ground staff to look after the many problems of handling passengers and their baggage at the airport. In addition, many airlines have their own training organizations which include sophisticated simulator systems for the constant checking and training required to keep a pilot's skills at the highest possible level. The large national airlines are almost invariably involved in the ownership of hotels and leisure complexes, holiday and travel agents, car hire companies and many other peripheral activities of the travel industry. They may also be involved in the maintenance and repair of aircraft, including their engines and avionics, belonging to other airlines as well as their own.

At the other end of the scale there will be small regional airlines, some with only one or two aircraft in their fleet but the remarkable fact in these cases is not the differences but the similarities of operation between large and small. The airline industry is a truly international brotherhood and every airline is, to some extent, dependent on others either as a provider of passengers or of services and expertise. Thus a small airline may be linked into a larger airline's computer reservation system (CRS), may have its aircraft maintained, its staff trained and even some of its routes provided by big brother. In return the major airline obtains a supply of passengers into its major hub, can delegate routes which could not be profitably operated by its own aircraft, and can defray some of its own expenses by charging for the use of facilities already in place for its own operation. For this type of symbiosis to exist, it is a prerequisite that airlines operate to common standards and use similar procedures for aircrew, engineers, and administrators. Thus in effect, each small airline is but a microcosm of the major air operators.

The result, of course, is not a boring conformity – as a glance through these pages will show. It is part of the airline business to project an image which will catch the public eye and persuade people to fly in their aircraft. One of the obvious manifestations of this is the great variety of aircraft liveries which can be seen at an airport and which is a source of endless fascination in its own right. The days are long gone when an airline would paint a red or blue stripe down the fuselage and put its name

in discreet letters on the side. Modern airlines often consult international design studios who consider not only aircraft color schemes but all aspects of the operation including uniforms, stationery, tickets, offices, catering and advertising in order to project an image of corporate efficiency and reliability. Occasionally the experts get it wrong. A few years ago a team of respected consultants charged British Airways a lot of money for ideas which included deleting the word Airways from the title painted on aircraft. While it might have seemed a good idea at the time, the result was people all over the world asking British What? It was quickly changed!

Nevertheless, the airline artist's job has perhaps grown easier as aircraft have changed. The modern jet airliner with its streamlined fuselage, upswept tall tailfin, and neatly podded engines clear of the swept-back wing, is a pleasing canvas to work on and there are some very striking results. As a general trend, airline liveries are becoming less intricate and designs are concentrating on simple, bold, and uncluttered markings. Many airlines, such as Air France, Quantas and Philippine Airlines, have followed a modern trend for a virtually all white fuselage relieved by colorful tail markings and the airline name on the side of the cabin. This type of marking is also suitable for the increasing number of airlines which do not own their aircraft but lease them from other operators or from the large leasing agencies. A simple livery can easily be changed when a leased aircraft moves to a new airline.

Other airlines still regard the use of color as necessary to project a 'quality image' and typical examples include British Airways, KLM, Northwest and Jordan's Alia who all go to great lengths to avoid the vast expanses of white which are so common elsewhere.

This pocket book can be regarded as a snapshot of the air transport industry at the start of the 1990s and it covers major aircraft together with a selection of the worlds airlines, majors and regionals alike. A browse through these pages will give the reader an overall impression of the state of the air transport industry today. Given the constant pressure for change within the airline industry, it is fascinating to speculate what a book such as this would contain in ten or even twenty years time. Look out for the next edition!

LEADING AIRLINERS

CONCORDE

The world's only successful supersonic airliner, Concorde has been in commercial service with Air France and British Airways since 1976. This Anglo/French project, begun in 1962, led to the flight of two prototypes in 1969 and two pre-production aircraft in 1971/72. The soaring cost of fuel in the early 1970s led to the cancellation of most orders and only 14 aircraft remain in service. BAe. and Aérospatiale are now considering a 250 passenger supersonic airliner for service entry in 2005.

SPECIFICATION

Type: Medium/long range supersonic airliner. 100 pax, First Class only seating.
Engines: Four Rolls Royce/SNECMA Olympus 593 Mk610 turbojets. 38,050 lb st with reheat.
Performance: Max cruise 1,176 kts at 51,000 ft. Range with max payload 3,360nm
Dimensions: Span 83ft 10in; length 203ft 9in; Wing 3,856 sq ft; ht 37ft 5in

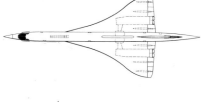

A300-600

The Airbus consortium was formed in 1970 in order to build European airliners to compete with the American giants. The first A300 flew in 1972 and production B2 models entered service with Air France in 1974. Next came the long range B4 and this was followed by the A300-600 in 1983 which utilised the ''glass cockpit'' pioneered by the smaller A310. The A300 has sold particularly well in the Far East and Pacific Rim countries and a total of 419 had been ordered by March 1991.

SPECIFICATION

Type: Medium/long range wide bodied airliner. Max 375 pax in 9 abreast seating
Engines: (-600) Two 56,000lb st Pratt & Whitney PW4156 or General Electric 58,900lb st CF6-80C2A1 turbofans
Performance: Max cruise 480 kts at 31,000 ft. Range with maximum payload 5,350mm
Dimensions: Span 147ft 1in; length 177ft 5in; Wing 2,799 sq ft; ht 54ft 6in

A310-300

Originally designated A300-B10, the A310 featured a shorter fuselage than its predecessor married to a new wing. More importantly this aircraft pioneered the use of CRT displays instead of conventional analogue instruments, reducing pilot workload and allowing a two pilot crew to become standard. Making its first flight in May 1982, the A310 entered service with launch customer Lufthansa in April 1983. Both the A300 and A310 were granted EROPS clearance for long overwater flights in 1990. By March 1991, orders for the A310 stood at 252.

SPECIFICATION

Type: Medium range wide bodied airliner Max 280 pax in 9 abreast seating
Engines: Two 53,500lb st General Electric CF6-50C2A2 or 52,000lb st Pratt & Whitney PW4156A turbofans
Performance: Max cruise 484 kts at 35,000ft. Range with maximum payload 6,900nm
Dimensions: Span 144ft; length 153ft 1 in; Wing 2,357 sq ft; ht 51ft 10in

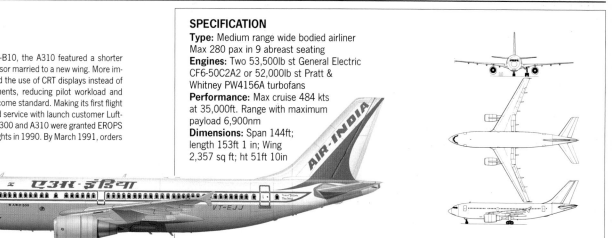

A320

Claimed to be the fastest selling airliner of all time, orders for the A320 and its derivatives reached 654 aircraft by early 1991. Considering that the first test and development aircraft only flew in 1987, this is an amazing achievement. The A320 is the first commercial airliner to feature "fly by wire" and all flight systems are computer controlled. A stretched version carrying 36 extra passengers and fitted with uprated engines is designated A321 while a shortened A319 carrying 130 passengers is under serious consideration.

SPECIFICATION

Type: Twin engined short range jet airliner. Max 179 pax in 6 abreast seating
Engines: Two 25,000lb st CFM56-5-A1 or, 26,500lb st CFM56-5-A3 or, 28,000lb st International Aero Engines IAE V2500 turbofans
Performance: Max cruise 487 kts at 28,000ft. Range with maximum payload 4,480nm
Dimensions: Span 119ft 9in; length 123ft 3in; Wing 1,320 sq ft; ht 38ft 8in

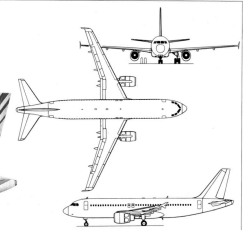

AIRBUS INDUSTRIE

ANTONOV

A340-200

Launched coincidently with the A330, the four engined A340 will fly first in late 1991, customer deliveries commencing in 1992. Airbus claim the A340 will hve the longest unrefuelled range of any airliner and many airlines are specifying a lower deck crew rest facility for use on flights which could last over 15 hours. Baseline version is the A340-200 while the -300 has a lengthened fuselage capable of carrying up to 440 passengers in a shorter range high density layout. 94 A340s ordered by March 1991.

SPECIFICATION
Type: Four engined very long range wide bodied airliner. Max 375 passengers
Engines: Four CFM International CFM56-5C-2 turbofans rated at 31,200lb st
Performance: Max cruise 500 kts at 33,000ft. Range with 262 pax, 7,550nm
Dimensions: Span 197ft 10in; length 194ft 10in; Wing 3,910 sq ft; ht 55ft 3in

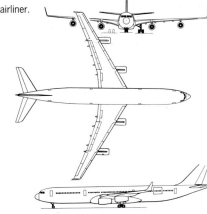

AN-24

The An-24 prototype flew in 1960 and entered service with Aeroflot in 1962. Since then over 1000 have been built including variants such as the An-24V which became the major production version, the An-24T freighter, and the An-24P for fire fighting duties. The RT and RV were fitted with a 1,984lb thrust auxiliary turbojet in the starboard nacelle to improve take off performance. Derivatives include the An-26 with a rear loading ramp and the An-30 while a modernised version is built in China as the Xian Y7-100.

SPECIFICATION
Type: Twin engined regional turboprop airliner. Max 50 pax in 4 abreast seating
Engines: Two 2,530 ehp Ivchenko A1-24A turboprops
Performance: Max cruise 269 kts. Range with max payload, 296nm. Max fuel range, 1,290nm
Dimensions: Span 95ft 9in; length 77ft 3in; Wing 807 sq ft; ht 27ft 3in

ATR42/72

This highly successful range of aircraft is a result of international collaboration between Alenia (previously Aeritalia) in Italy and érospatiale in France to produce an Avion de Transport Regionale (ATR). The ATR42 first flew in 1984 with the stretched ATR72 following four years later. Both aircraft are available in high gross weight nd dedicated freight versions while the PW127 powered ATR72-10 was launched at the end of 1990 following a large order the merican Eagle network. Over 400 ATR42/72 have been ordered.

SPECIFICATION
Type: Twin turboprop regional airliner. Max 50 (ATR42) or 74 (ATR72) passengers
Engines: ATR42; two Pratt & Whitney PW120 turboprops rated at 1,800 shp. ATR72;two PW124B turboprops rated at 2,400 shp
Performance: Max cruise 266kts (283 kts ATR72). Range 970nm with 48 pax (1500nm/66pax ATR72)
Dimensions: ATR42 Span 80ft 7in; length 74ft 5in; wing 586.6 sq ft; ht 24ft 11in

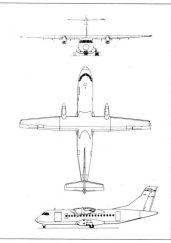

707-320

Although the Comet was the first jet airliner, the Boeing 707 with its highly swept wings and neatly podded engines completely utclassed the British aircraft when it began commercial flights with an Am in 1958. Early 707-120s were used for transatlantic flights ut the first true intercontinental model was the stretched 707-320. 25 707s were built, the last commercial example being delivered 1982. The Boeing 720 was a redesign of the 707 airframe intended for use on short/medium range routes. 154 were built.

SPECIFICATION
Type: Four engined long range jet airliner. Max 188 passengers in 6 abreast seating
Engines: Four 18,000lb st Pratt & Whitney JT3D-3 or 19,000lb st JT3D-7 turbofans. 707-420 powered by 17,500lb st Rolls Royce Conway 508 Turbofans
Performance: Max cruise 516 kts at 30,000ft. Range with max payload 5,175nm
Dimensions: Span 145ft 9in; length 152ft 9in; Wing 2,892 sq ft; ht 42ft 6in

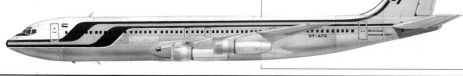

BOEING

727-200

The original 131 seater 727-100 flew in February 1963 and was followed by the stretched 727-200 in 1967. Maximum take off weight rose from 160,000lb to 175,000lb, while the Advanced 727-200 introduced in 1972 allowed a further increase to 209,500lb, although maximum seating remained at 189. A total of 1,831 727s of all versions had been delivered when production ceased in 1984. Currently Valsan and Dee Howard offer re-engined and modernised 727s to meet current noise regulations and improve fuel efficiency.

SPECIFICATION
Type: Short/medium range jet airliner. Max 189 pax in 6 abreast seating
Engines: Three 14,500-17,400lb st Pratt & Whitney JT8D series turbofans
Performance: Max cruise 523 kts at 25,000ft. Range with maximum payload 2,615nm
Dimensions: Span 108ft; length 153ft 2in; Wing 1,650 sq ft; ht 34ft

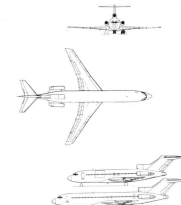

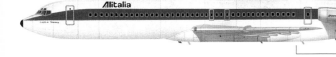

737-400

The 737-400 is the largest version of the world's best selling airliner. First flown in 1967 the original short fuselage 737-100 was quickly replaced by the slightly larger 737-200 which flew later the same year. In 1981 Boeing launched the stretched 149 seater 737-300 with CFM56-3B turbofans replacing the previous JT8Ds and advanced avionics on the flightdeck. The 737-400 was a further stretch to carry up to 188 passengers while the smaller 737-500, also powered by CFM56 engines replaced the -200 series in production.

SPECIFICATION
Type: Twin engined short/medium range jet airliner. Max 168 pax in 6 abreast seating Two CFM International 22,000lb st CFM56-3-B2 or 23,500lb st CFM56-3C turbofans
Performance: Max cruise 492 kts at 26,000ft. Range with Maximum payload 3,611nm
Dimensions: Span 94ft 9in; length 119ft 7in; Wing 1,135 sq ft; ht 36ft 6in

747-400

Boeing's mighty 747 is the aircraft which transformed modern air travel. First flown in 1969, commercial services with launch customer Pan Am began in 1970. Development of the original 747-200 led to the higher gross weight -200B, the short fuselage long range SP and short range high capacity SR. The -300 introduced a stretched upper deck while the -400 is an extensive redesign with advanced avionics and aerodynamic improvements including distinctive upturned winglets. All major variants have been produced in cargo and Combi versions.

SPECIFICATION

Type: Four engine very long range widebody airliner. 412 pax in mixed class layout
Engines: Four Gen. Electric CF6-80C2 or Pratt & Whitney PW4056 or Rolls Royce Trent RB211-534G/H turbofans.
Performance: Max cruise 507 kts at 35,000ft. Range 7,300nm
Dimensions: Span 211ft 5in; length 231ft 10in; Wing 5,650 sq ft; ht 64ft 4in

757-200

Intended as a replacement for the successful but fuel thirsty 727, the prototype 757 flew in 1982 and Eastern Airlines began airline services in January 1983. Initially sales were disappointing by Boeing standards but the air travel boom in the mid 1980s led to a succession of orders and 724 had been ordered by early 1991. Unusually there have been few derivative versions of the basic 757-200, these being confined to the 757PF parcels freighter and the 757M Combi.

SPECIFICATION

Type: Twin engine medium range jet airliner. Max 239 pax in 6 abreast seating.
Engines: Two 40,100lb st Rolls Royce RB211-535C or -535E4, or Pratt & Whitney 38,200lb st PW2037 or 41,700lb st PW2040 turbofans
Performance: Max cruise 505 kts at 31,000ft. Range with 186 pax, 3,910nm (high gross wt option)
Dimensions: Span 124ft 10in; length 155ft 3in; Wing 1994 sq ft; ht 44ft 6in

BOEING

767-300

Developed in parallel with the 757, the larger 767 was the first to fly – in 1981. Both aircraft share many features including an identical flightdeck which eases pilot training requirements. The basic 300,000lb gross weight 767-200 was quickly followed by the 350,000lb stretched 767-300 which flew in 1986. Most recent orders are for the Extended Range -200ER and -300ER which have a further weight increase to carry more fuel and modifications to permit long overwater EROPS flights. Total orders stand at 565 in mid 1991.

SPECIFICATION
Type: Twin engined medium/long range jet airliner. Max 290 pax in 7 abreast layout
Engines: Two General Electric 53,000lb st CF6-80C2B2 or, 53,000lb st Pratt & Whitney PW4050 turbofans
Performance: Max cruise 489 kts at 39,000ft. Range 4000nm with 210 pax in mixed class
Dimensions: Span 156ft 1in; length 180ft 3in; Wing 3,050ft; ht 52ft

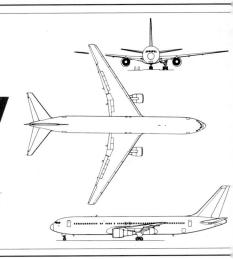

Britannia G-BKPW

777

Boeing's latest airliner was originally conceived as a further stretch of the 767 but consultation with major airlines led to the launch of an all new 777 in October 1990 and first flight is planned for 1994. Firm orders to date include United Airlines (34), All Nippon (15), British Airways (15), Thai Airways (6). A unique option is folding wingtips, reducing span to 156ft for ground manoeuvring at crowded airports. Future developments will include a long range version able to carry 300 passengers over 6,600nm.

SPECIFICATION
Type: Twin engine long range widebody airliner. Max 440 pax in 10 abreast layout
Engines: Two General Electric GE90 (75,000-85,000lb st) or Pratt & Whitney PW4073 (73,000-84,500lb st) or Rolls Royce Trent 871/872 (75,000 to 85,000) turbofans
Performance: Max cruise 490 kts at 31,000ft. Range 4,800 miles with 360 pax
Dimensions: Span 196ft 11in; length 209ft 1in; height 60ft

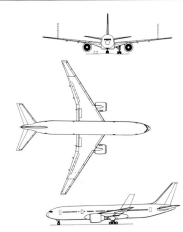

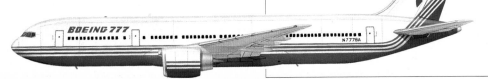

BOEING 777 N7778A

BAC-111-500

Originally developed by the British Aircraft Corporation, the prototype BAC-111 flew in August 1963 and 232 had been built when UK production ceased in 1982. Variants included the externally similar 200, 300 and 400 series while the 500 featured a lengthened fuselage and extended wings. The 475 retained a short fuselage with the new wing and more powerful engines: Spey powered 111s were built under licence by Rombac/CNIAR in Roumania, but future plans envisage production of the Tay powered Series 2000.

SPECIFICATION
Type: Twin engined short range jet airliner. Max 119 pax in 5 abreast seating
Engines: Two 12,550lb st Rolls Royce Spey 512-14DW turbofans
Performance: Max cruise 457 kts at 30,000ft. Range with maximum payload, 1,500 nm
Dimensions: Span 93ft 6in; length 107ft; wing 1,031 sq ft; ht 24ft 6in

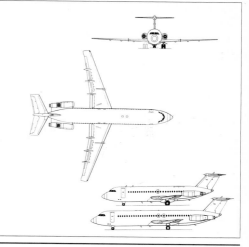

146-300

With around 300 aircraft on order, the BAe.146 is now Britain's most successful jet airliner. The 146-100 first flew in 1981 and was followed by the successively larger -200 and -300 in 1982 and 1987. A freighter version, 146QT (Quiet Trader), has been ordered in large numbers by the Australian based TNT group. The RJ70 and RJ80 are lightweight versions of the 146-100 with derated engines. Also projected is the 146NRA, a 130 seater twin CFM56 powered version.

SPECIFICATION
Type: Four engined short-medium range jet airliner. 103-122 seats, 5/6 abreast
Engines: Four 6,970lb st Textron Lycoming ALF502R-5 or 7,000lb st LF507 turbofans
Performance: Max cruise 429 kts at 26,000ft. Range with maximum payload 1,090nm
Dimensions: Span 86ft 5in; length 101ft 8in; wing 832 sq ft; ht 15ft 6in

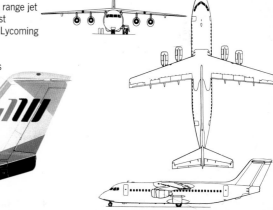

BRITISH AEROSPACE

BOEING CANADA

ATP

The above data applies to the ATP which first flew in August 1986 and BAe. currently hold orders or options for 78 aircraft. The ATP is a direct derivative of the Dart powered 48 seater Avro/HS748 of which 382 (including military and licence built versions) were sold between 1960 and 1988 when production ceased. Compared to the 748, the ATP has an 18ft fuselage extension, modern fuel efficient PW124/126 turboprops, some aerodynamic changes including a swept tailfin and advanced avionics on the flightdeck.

SPECIFICATION

Type: Twin engined turboprop regional airliner. 64-72 seats in 4 abreast layout
Engines: Two 2,653shp Pratt & Whitney Canada PW126A turboprops
Performance: Max cruise 265 ktsat 13,000ft. Max range with 64 pax, 930nm
Dimensions: Span 100ft 6in; length 85ft 4in; wing 843 sq ft; ht 24ft 11in

DASH 7

The rugged Dash 7 is unique among modern airliners with its ability to lift a full load from small airstrips and airports such as London's City Airport, sited on a converted dockside. 111 Dash 7s had been built by de Havilland Canada when production ceased in 1988, by which time the company had become a division of Boeing. Developments of the basic 100 series aircraft were a cargo version (101), the Dash 7R for the Canadian Coastguard, and the 150/151 with increased gross weight and extra fuel capacity.

SPECIFICATION

Type: Four engined short range STOL turboprop airliner. 44-54 passengers
Engines: Four 1,120shp Pratt & Whitney Canada PT6A-50 turboprops
Performance: Max cruise 230 kts at 10,000ft. Range with maximum payload 530nm
Dimensions: Span 93ft; length 80ft 8in; wing 860 sq ft; ht 26ft 2in

BOEING CANADA

CANADAIR

DASH 8-100

Conceived as a smaller partner to the Dash 7, the twin engined Dash 8 has proved to be more successful and in its -300 version can carry the same passenger load faster, higher, further and at less cost. The prototype Dash 8-100 flew in 1983 and the -300, with a 10 foot fuselage stretch and PW123 turboprops, flew in 1987. Over 360 aircraft of both versions have been ordered. A projected 64/70 seater Dash 8-400 is unlikely to go ahead following the sale of the company to the rival ATR group.

SPECIFICATION

Type: Twin turboprop short range regional airliner. 36-40 seats, 4 abreast layout
Engines: Two 2,150 shp Pratt & Whitney Canada PW120A turboprops
Performance: Max cruise 271 kts at 15,000ft. Range with maximum payload 840nm
Dimensions: Span 85ft; length 73ft; wing area 585 sq ft; ht 24ft 7in

REGIONAL JET

Canadair's RJ (Regional Jet) is derived from the Challenger 601 executive jet although with a 20 foot fuselage stretch, increased wing area, uprated engines and new avionics the similarities are only superficial. Following the first flight in May 1991, production deliveries to the launch customer, German regional DLT, will begin in late 1992. These aircraft will be the series 100ER with higher gross weight allowing increased fuel and range. Future plans include the 70-74 seater series 200 with uprated CF34 turbofans.

SPECIFICATION

Type: Twin engined regional jet airliner. 50-54 seats, 4 abreast layout
Engines: Two 9,220lb st General Electric CF34-3A turbofans
Performance: Max cruise 459 kts at 37,000ft. Max range with 50 pax, 1,418nm
Dimensions: Span 70ft 4in; length 88ft 5in; wing 581 sq ft; ht 20ft 8in

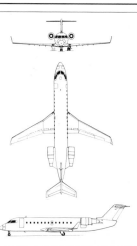

CN-235

The CN-235 is the product of a collaborative programme between CASA of Spain and IPTN of Indonesia who have formed a joint company, Airtech, responsible for production and sales. Parallel production facilities have been set up in both countries, each factory flying its first aircraft in 1983. Since then the CN-235 has sold steadily with over 140 orders from civil and military customers including the Iberia subsidiary Binter, and Merpati and Pelita AS in Indonesia. IPTN are now developing the larger N-250.

SPECIFICATION
Type: Twin engined turboprop regional airliner. Max 45 pax in 4 abreast layout
Engines: Two 1,750/1,870 shp General Electric CT7-9C turboprops
Performance: Max cruise 248 kts at 15,000ft. Range with maximum payload 750nm
Dimensions: Span 84ft 8in; length 70ft 1in; wing 636 sq ft; ht 26ft 10in

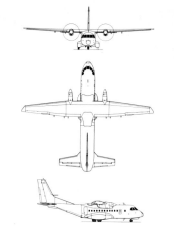

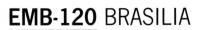

EMB-120 BRASILIA

Based in Brazil, Embraer are one of the world's major producers of commuter airliners. Following the successful 18 seater Bandierante, of which 500 were sold, Embraer launched the pressurised 30 seater Brasilia in 1979 and test flying commenced in 1983. With its high performance and comfortable cabin, the aircraft proved popular with several US airlines while DLT were the first European operator, in 1986. To date over 500 orders and options have been announced. The EMB-145 is a projected 45 seat jet powered derivative.

SPECIFICATION
Type: Twin engined turboprop regional airliner. 30 pax in 3 abreast layout
Engines: Two 1,800shp Pratt & Whitney Canada PW118 turboprops
Performance: Max cruise 315 kts at 25,000ft. Range with maximum payload 300nm
Dimensions: Span 64ft 11in; length 65ft 7in; wing 424 sq ft; ht 20ft 10in

50/F27 FRIENDSHIP

Powered by the ubiquitous Rolls Royce Dart turboprop, the worldbeating Fokker F27 first flew in 1955. Subsequently 786 were built up to 1987 when production ceased and the 48 seater F27 is still widely used. Despite a similar appearance, the new Fokker 50 incorporates major changes including PW125B turboprops, new cabin and flightdeck, new aircraft systems and aerodynamic improvements. Since first flight in 1985, 130 firm orders have been placed. A stretched 68 seater Fokker 50 series 400 is planned.

SPECIFICATION

Type: Twin engined short range turboprop airliner. 46-58 seats, 4 abreast layout
Engines: Two 2,250/2,500 shp Pratt & Whitney Canada PW125B turboprops
Performance: Max cruise 282 kts at 16,000ft. Range with 50 pax 1,635nm
Dimensions: Span 95ft 3in; length 82ft 10in; wing 7,535 sq ft; ht 27ft 4in

(Data refers to Fokker 50)

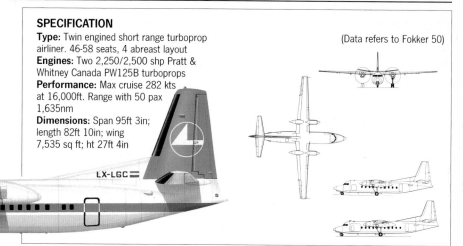

100/F28 FELLOWSHIP

Fokker sold 241 F28 Fellowships between 1967 and 1986, when production ceased. Powered by Rolls Royce Spey turbofans, the aircraft grew from the 65 seater Mk.1000 to the 85 seater 73,000lb gross weight Mk.4000. Further demand for growth led to the completely revised Fokker 100 with a substantial fuselage stretch and more efficient Tay engines. By mid 1991 Fokker held orders and options for 351 aircraft. Recently announced are the 77 seater Fokker 80 and 137 seater Fokker 130 for delivery in 1996/97.

SPECIFICATION

Type: Twin engine short range jet airliner. 97-122 seats, 5 abreast layout.
Engines: Two Rolls Royce Tay 620-15 (13,850lb st) or Tay 650-15 (15,100lb st) turbofans
Performance: Max cruise 459 kts at 27,000ft. Max range with 107 pax, 1,615nm
Dimensions: Span 92ft 1in; length 106ft 8in; wing 1,006 sq ft; ht 27ft 10in

(Data refers to Fokker 100)

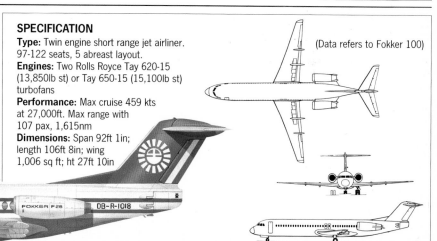

ILYUSHIN

Il-62MK

Bearing a marked resemblance to the contemporary British VC-10, the Il-62 first flew in 1963 and the initial production version which entered service with Aeroflot in 1967 was powered by 23,000lb thrust Kuznetsov NK-8-4 turbofans. The Il-62M, powered by Soliviev D-30 engines, came into service in 1974 and the higher gross weight Il-62MK followed four years later. Approximately 240 are believed to have been produced, including several for export, and current operators include Aeroflot, Cubana, LAM and Tarom.

SPECIFICATION
Type: Four engine long range jet airliner 174 pax in two cabin 6 abreast layout
Engines: Four 24,400lb st Soloviev D-30KU turbofans
Performance: Max cruise 496 kts at 26,000ft. Range with maximum payload 4,200nm
Dimensions: Span 141ft 9in; length 174ft 3in; wing 3,009 sq ft; ht 40ft 6in

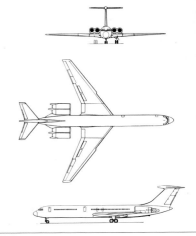

Il-86

This aircraft was the first Soviet designed widebody airliner to enter service but it would appear that it has not been a technical success, suffering from poor payload range performance. To improve matters it is planned to re-engine the aircraft with Soloviev PS90A turbofans and service entry of this version is imminent. In the longer term the possibility of fitting CFM56 turbofans is also being considered, as is the introduction of "glass cockpit" technology. Approximately 100 Il-86s are believed to be on order.

SPECIFICATION
Type: Four engine medium range widebody jet airliner. Max 350 pax in 9 abreast seats
Engines: Two 28,660lb st Kuznetsov NK-86 turbofans
Performance: Max cruise 512 kts at 35,000ft. Range with maximum payload 1,250nm
Dimensions: Span 157ft 8in; length 195ft 4in; wing 3,444 sq ft; ht 51ft 10in

ILYUSHIN

Il-96-300

Although similar in outline to the Il-86, the Il-96 is a much more advanced aircraft and is the first Soviet airliner to feature "fly by wire". First flown in 1988, the Il-96-300 will enter service during 1991 and a stretched long range version, the Il-96M, is currently under development. Powered by Pratt & Whitney 37,000lb thrust PW2337 turbofans it will have a range of 7,000nm carrying over 300 passengers. Also planned is a twin engined variant powered by either PW4000s or RR Trents.

SPECIFICATION

Type: Four engine long range widebody jet airliner. Max 300 pax in 9 abreast seats
Engines: Four 35,000lb st Soloviev PS-90A turbofans. Projected Il-96M to be powered by Pratt & Whitney PW2037 turbofans.
Performance: Max cruise 480 kts at 35,000ft. Range with maximum payload 4,860nm
Dimensions: Span 189ft 2in; length 181ft 7in; wing 4,215 sq ft; ht 57ft 8in

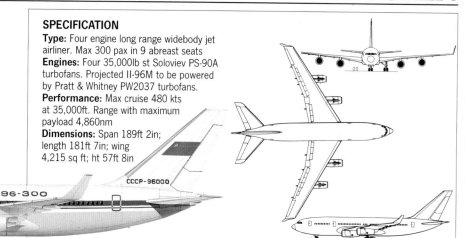

ILYUSHIN Il-114

Flown for the first time on 29 March 1990, the Il-114 is destined for large scale production. Deliveries are expected to commence in 1992 to meet an expected Aeroflot requirement for 500 aircraft. The flightdeck uses modern CRT displays and American companies have won orders to supply avionic equipment. In outline the Il-114 bears more than a passing resemblance to the ATP and it is interesting to recall that BAe. had at one stage discussed plans for producing the ATP in Russia.

SPECIFICATION

Type: Twin engined regional turboprop airliner. 60-68 seats, 4 abreast layout
Engines: Two 2,500shp Isotov TV7-117 turboprops
Performance: Max cruise 270 kts at 26,000ft. Range with maximum payload 450nm
Dimensions: Span 98ft 5in; length 86ft 4in; height 30ft 7in

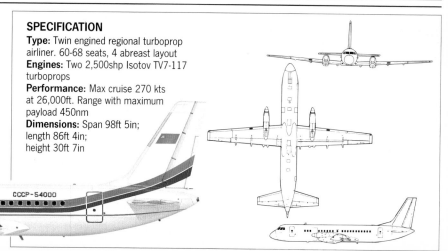

LOCKHEED

MCDONNELL DOUGLAS

L-1011-500 TRISTAR

The Tristar was one of the aircraft which launched the widebody era at the beginning of the 1970s and was produced in several versions, all powered by Rolls Royce RB211 engines. The initial -1 model, which first flew in 1970, was followed by the -100 with extra fuel capacity for increased range, and the -200 with more powerful engines for improved performance. 1978 saw the introduction of the short fuselage long range -500. Production ended in 1984 after 250 Tristars had been built.

SPECIFICATION

Type: Three engined long range widebody jet airliner. Max 330 pax in 10 abreast layout
Engines: Three 50,000lb st Rolls Royce RB211-524B turbofans
Performance: Max cruise 518 kts at 30,000ft. Range with maximum payload 5,098nm
Dimensions: Span 164ft 4in; length 164ft 3in; wing 3,540 sq ft; ht 55ft 4in

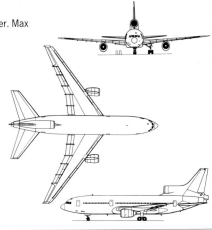

DC-8-73

The DC-8 first flew in 1958 and was a contemporary and rival of the Boeing 707 and 556 were built, production ceasing in 1972. The last versions to be built were the long range stretched Series 60 aircraft which could carry up to 259 passengers. From 1982 onwards 66 of these latter aircraft were re-engined with the CFM56-2 by Cammacorp and were recertificated as DC-8-70 series. Customers for these conversions, which produced fuel savings of 23%, included Air Canada, Delta, Minerve, and UPS.

SPECIFICATION

Type: Four engined long range jet airliner. Max 269 pax in 6 abreast seating
Engines: Four CFM International 22,000lb st CFM56-2-C5 turbofans
Performance: Max cruise 479 kts at 39,000ft. Range with maximum payload 4,200nm
Dimensions: Span 148ft 5in; length 187ft 5in; wing 2,927 sq ft; ht 43ft

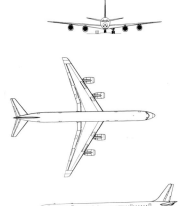

DC-9-30

One of the most popular airliners ever built, no less than 976 DC-9s in five basic versions were produced before it was superseded in the early 1980s by the MD-80 series. Following the original DC-9-10 came the -30 with longer fuselage, increased span and uprated engines; the -20 was similar but without the fuselage stretch; the -40 was a 125 seater ordered by SAS and the -50 featured yet further lengthening, at the request of Swissair, to seat 139 passengers.

SPECIFICATION

Type: Twin engined short/medium range jet airliner. Max 115 pax in 5 abreast seats
Engines: Two 15,500lb st Pratt & Whitney JT8D-15 turbofans
Performance: Max cruise 503 kts at 26,000ft. Range with maximum payload 1,576nm
Dimensions: Span 93ft 4in; length 119ft 4in; wing 1,001 sq ft; ht 27ft 5in

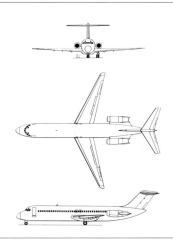

DC-10-30

A contemporary of the Tristar, the DC-10 was a greater commercial success and remained in production until 1989. A total of 446 was built, including 60 KC-10 tankers for the USAF. Main civil versions were the DC-10-10 for high density short/medium range routes and the long range DC-10-30 with uprated engines and increased gross weight, the latter necessitating a third main undercarriage unit centrally mounted under the fuselage. The -40 was similar to the -30 but was powered by JT9D engines.

SPECIFICATION

Type: Three engined long range widebody jet airliner. Max 380 pax in 10 abreast seats
Engines: Three 52,500lb st General Electric CF6-50C1 turbofans. Series 40 powered by 53,000lb Pratt & Whitney JT9D-59A turbofans
Performance: Max cruise 516 kts at 31,000ft. Range with maximum payload 5,380nm
Dimensions: Span 165ft 4in; length 181ft 7in; wing 3,958 sq ft; ht 58ft 1in

MCDONNELL DOUGLAS

MD-11

Derived from the DC-10, the MD-11 first flew in 1990. Production has built up rapidly and the aircraft is now in service with Finnair, Delta, Korean, Swissair and Thai International. The basic MD-11 is almost 19ft longer than the DC-10 and features new engines, improved aerodynamics and a sophisticated "glass cockpit". The MD-11F Freighter is in service with Federal Express and a Combi version is also available. Work is already underway on a stretched version known as the MD-12.

SPECIFICATION

Type: Three engine very long range widebody jet airliner. Max 405 passengers
Engines: Three 61,500lb st General Electric CF6-80C2-D1F or 60,000lb st P & W PW4460
Performance: Max cruise 510 kts at 31,000ft. Max range, with 293 passengers, 8,040nm
Dimensions: Span 169 ft 6in; length 200ft 10in; wing 3,648 sq ft; ht 57ft 9in

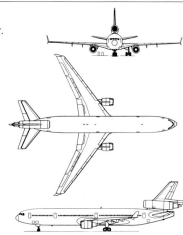

MD-83

The MD-80 was originally flown as the DC-9 Super 80 in 1979, the main changes being a greatly lengthened fuselage to carry 179 passengers and the installation of fuel efficient JT8D-200 series engines. There are several variants and the MD81/82/83 are of similar size with alternative engines, fuel loads and gross weights. The MD87 is short fuselage 130-seater and the MD-88 features electronic flight instrumentation. Due to fly in 1993 is the first of the MD-90 family powered by IAE V2500 engines.

SPECIFICATION

Type: Twin engined short/medium range jet airliner. Max 172 pax, 5 abreast layout
Engines: Two 21,000lb st Pratt & Whitney JT8D-219 turbofans
Performance: Max cruise 499 kts at 27,000ft. Range with maximum payload 2,375nm
Dimensions: Span 107ft 8in; length 147ft 9in; wing 1,270 sq ft; ht 29ft 6in

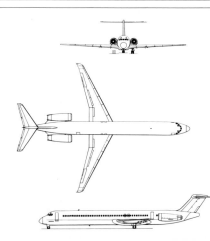

340B and 2000

The 340 was initially a joint venture, launched in 1979, between Saab and Fairchild but the American company withdrew in 1985 and all production is centred at Linköping in Sweden. The prototype 340 flew in 1983, deliveries to Crossair started in 1984 and over 200 are now in service. Current production model is the 340B with uprated engines. Due to fly in 1992 is the 50 seat Saab 2000 which will cruise at 360 kts, giving block times comparable to the new generation of Regional Jets.

SPECIFICATION

Type: Twin engine turboprop regional airliner. 35-37 seats in 3 abreast layout
Engines: Two 1,870shp General Electric CT7-9B turboprops. SAAB 2000 powered by two 3,285 shp Allison GMA 2100 turboprops
Performance: Max cruise 282 kts at 15,000ft. Range with maximum payload 643nm
Dimensions: Span 70ft 4in; length 64ft 8in; wing 450 sq ft; ht 22ft 6in •

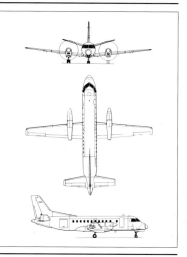

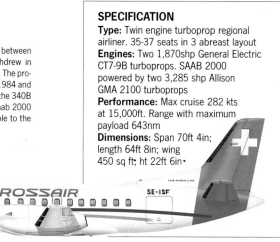

330 and 360

Affectionately known as "Sheds", these rugged commuter airliners have been in service since 1976 and approximately 370 of all versions, including military, have been sold. The 330, instantly recognisable by virtue of its twin tail fins, carries 30 passengers while the lengthened 360 carries up to 36 in standard layout and features a redesigned tail with a single swept fin. Both aircraft share the same square section unpressurised cabin with full standing headroom. Current production centres on the 360-300.

SPECIFICATION

Type: Twin engined turboprop commuter airliner. 36-39 seats in 3 abreast layout
Engines: Two 1,424 shp Pratt & Whitney PT6A-65AR turboprops. Shorts 330 powered by two PT6A-45A/B or R turboprops
Performance: Max cruise 190 kts at 10,000ft. Range with maximum payload 473nm
Dimensions: Span 74ft 10in; length 70ft 10in; wing 453 sq ft; ht 23ft 10in

(Data refers to Shorts 360)

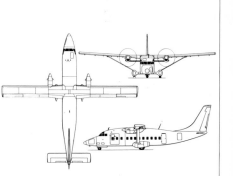

TUPOLEV

TU-154B-2

Making its first flight in 1968, the Tu-154 subsequently became the backbone of the Aeroflot fleet and has been widely exported. The original Tu-154A was followed by the Tu-154B and B-2 in 1977 and an all cargo version was also produced. Amazingly this venerable design is still in production as the Tu-154M which entered service in 1984, Sloviev D-30KU turbofans replacing the less efficient Kuznetsov NK-8s. Almost 700 Tu-154s have been produced and most remain in service today.

SPECIFICATION
Type: Three engine medium range jet airliner. Max 180 pax in 6 abreast layout
Engines: Three 23,150lb st Kuznetsov KN-8-2U turbofans or (Tu-154M) three 23,380lb st Soloviev DO30KU-154-II turbofans
Performance: Max cruise 514 kts at 31,000ft. Range with maximum payload 2,100nm
Dimensions: Span 123ft 2in; length 157ft 2in; wing 2,169; ht 37ft 5in

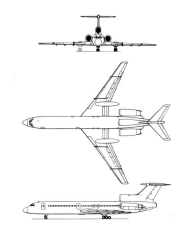

TU-204

Bearing an almost uncanny resemblance to the Boeing 757, the Tu-204 is intended as a replacement for the Tu-154. First flown in January 1989, the aircraft is equipped with a digital "Fly by Wire" system and advanced electronic flight deck displays. Powered by Soloviev PS-90A turbofans, the Tu-204 burns almost 40% more fuel per passenger than its western counterpart. Consequently the Tu-204-200 will be powered by Rolls Royce RB211-535E5/F5 engines which may well transform the aircraft into a serious contender for orders from western airlines.

SPECIFICATION
Type: Twin engine medium range jet airliner. Max 219 pax in 6 abreast seating
Engines: Two 35,500st Soloviev PS-90A turbofans. Also projected, two 40,000lb st Rolls Royce RB211-535E4
Performance: Max cruise 486 kts at 35,000ft. Range with maximum payload 1,350nm
Dimensions: Span 137ft 9in; length 151ft 8in; wing 1,983 sq ft; ht 45ft 7in

YAK-42

This attractive looking trijet has had a chequered career since it first flew in 1975. Entering service in 1980 with Aeroflot, it was withdrawn between 1982 and 1984 due to technical problems. Standard production model, introduced in 1990, is the Yak-42D with extra fuel capacity and increased gross weight. It has been sold China, India and Italy. The 168 seater Yak-42M is under development and will have new engines, a supercritical wing with winglets, electronic flightdeck displays and fly by wire controls.

SPECIFICATION

Type: Three engined short/medium range jet airliner. Max 120 pax in 6 abreast seats
Engines: Three 14,330lb st Lotarev D-36 turbofans
Performance: Max cruise 437 kts at 25,000ft. Range with maximum payload 1,025nm
Dimensions: Span 114ft 5in; length 119ft 4in; wing 1,615 sq ft; ht 32ft 3in

GLOSSARY

ATP Advanced Turboprop

block times The measure applied to the time taken for an aircraft to carry out a given flight from take off to touchdown including an allowance for such factors as speed restrictions and holding procedures.

Combi A version of a passenger airliner modified to simultaneously carry a mix of passengers and cargo on its main deck (note that almost all large airliners can carry cargo in their underfloor holds).

CRT Cathode ray tube

ehp Effective horsepower

ER Extended Range. A term generally applied to versions of an aircraft certificated for EROPS(cf)

EROPS Extended Range Operations. Refers to rules governing the use of twin engined aircraft on long overwater routes. Normally the aircraft must be flown so that it can reach a suitable diversion airfield within a specified time (normally 120 or 180 minutes) at single engine flying speed in the event of the failure of one engine.

Fly By Wire A system whereby the pilot's control inputs are processed by flight computer before being signalled to the moving flying control surfaces on the wing and tail. This is designed to ensure that the aircraft cannot exceed its safe flying parameters.

ft Feet. 1 foot = 305mm

glass cockpit Term used to describe a modern aircraft flightdeck where traditional instruments and dials have been replaced by electronic displays.

ht Height

IAE International Aero Engines. An international consortium responsible for the design and production of the V2500 turbofan and other engines.

in Inch. 1 inch = 25mm

kts Knots = nautical miles per hour.

lb Pound weight. 1lb = 0.4536Kg

max Maximum

nm Nautical miles. 1 nautical mile = 6080 ft

pax Passengers. Capacities quoted in these tables are generally the maximum which can be accommodated but most airliners, particularly the larger ones, are normally flown in a mixed class configuration which considerably reduces the number of seats available.

RJ Regional Jet

shp Shaft horsepower

SNECMA Société Nationale d'Étude et de Construction de Moteurs d'Aviation. Producers of the CFM56 turbofan in co-operation with General Electric.

sq.ft Square feet

st Static Thrust

STOL Short Take Off and Landing

turbofan A type of jet engine where a high proportion of the air drawn in by the compressor fan assembly bypasses the main core of the engine and does not go through the combustion and turbine stages. This type of engine has exceptionally good fuel efficiency.

Wing Wing Area

Aer Lingus

The flag carrier of The Republic of Ireland began operations in April 1936, opening the first scheduled passenger service between Eire and Great Britain. It was flown from Dublin to Bristol by a DH 84 Dragon. Later that year the service was extended to London and Aer Lingus established a monopoly of air routes between the United Kingdom and Ireland. Throughout the war years an air link across the Irish Sea was maintained by Aer Lingus between Dublin and either Liverpool or Manchester.

The acquisition of DC-3s in 1948 allowed routes to be opened up linking Dublin directly with the continent of Europe, with services to Paris and Amsterdam. Aer Lingus was one of the first airlines to operate an all turbine-powered fleet, swapping its DC-3s in 1959 for Fokker F27s, which joined eight Viscount 808s. The airline was subsequently an early customer for the BAC.111 and the Boeing 737.

In 1958 a second airline, called Aerlinte Eireann (Irish International Airlines), also owned by the state holding company, Air Rianta, was put into operation. It provided a transatlantic service using L-1049H Lockheed Constellations (leased from Seaboard and Western) flying to New York and Boston with their large ethnic Irish populations. In 1960 the Constellations were replaced by Boeing 720-048s. The activities of Aerlinte Eireann were later merged with those of Aer Lingus. Current long-haul equipment consists of three Boeing 747s. Two leased Boeing 767-300ER were introduced in 1991 but due to the slump in traffic, were sub leased to another airline.

Today, after a policy decision taken in the late 1970s to diversify business activities, the company has several important subsidiaries operating in hotels, leisure and contract air transport and airport services. Associated firms include Irish Helicopters, Guinness Peat Aviation (the biggest aircraft leasing company in the world), Air Tara and Air Taras Teo – a cargo airline with three DC-8s. Team Aer Lingus is a recently formed company which will handle all the airline's major engineering as well as providing services for other operations. A $60 million investment includes a massive new hangar at Dublin, capable of holding two Boeing 747-400 and four narrow bodies. This was completed in 1991.

Scheduled passenger and freight services are operated from Dublin to London (Heathrow and Gatwick), Birmingham, Bristol, East Midlands, Edinburgh, Glasgow, Leeds/Bradford, Manchester, Jersey, Paris, Brussels, Amsterdam, Copenhagen, Düsseldorf, Frankfurt, Zurich, Rome, Madrid, Milan, New York, Boston and Chicago. Domestic links are

flown to Cork, Connaught Regional airport, Derry, Kerry County, Shannon and Waterford. From Cork airport services are flown to London, Jersey, Amsterdam, Dublin, Paris, Bristol and Rennes.

And from Shannon on the west coast scheduled passenger services are operated to London, Amsterdam, Dublin, Paris, New York, Boston and Chicago. The airline also offers services from Manchester to Amsterdam, Copenhagen, Hamburg and Zurich in a fifth freedom operation made possible by EC deregulation.

The fully owned subsidiary, Aer Lingus Commuter, was established in 1984 and operates a fleet of twin-prop Fokker 50s and Shorts 360s on domestic routes and to Bristol, East Midlands, Edinburgh, Leeds/ Bradford, Newcastle, Bristol and Manchester in the UK and Rennes in Brittany. The Shorts will be replaced by 5 Saab 340s during 1991.

Fleet: three Boeing 747-100, one Boeing 767-300ER, 11 Boeing 737-200, two Boeing 737-300, four 737-400, five Boeing 737-500; four BAe One-Eleven 200 (for sale); one Lockheed L-1011 (on lease). On order 4 Boeing 737-500, one 767-300ER.
Fleet (Air Lingus Commuter): six Fokker 50; five Shorts 360. On order, five Saab 340.

Above, left
A Boeing 737 prepares for take-off
Above
A Shorts 360 of Aer Lingus Commuter

Below
Vickers Viscount 808s were operated by Aer Lingus in the late 1950s

Aeroflot (GRAZHDENSKY VOZDUSHNY FLOT)

Much of the history of the biggest civil aircraft operator in the world remain wreathed in mystery because of its close integration with the Soviet armed forces and the strategic interests of the state. The exact composition of its fleet still remains secret. With a huge internal market – Aeroflot carries 10% of the world's air travelers – backed by a massive and technologically competitive civil aircraft industry, the airline should be a global supercarrier. Yet today Aeroflot reflects the economic turmoil and quest for new commercial mechanisms in the Soviet Union as a whole.

The reform plan of 1988, to break the giant up into divisional profit centers – involving joint marketing deals with world airlines in a bid to compete internationally with western standards of service and technical efficiency, appeared to come to a halt at the outset of 1991.

The airline was founded soon after the birth of the Soviet state. In 1923 the Civil Aviation Council was formed to operate the new state airline, Dobrolet. Two years later Dobrolet swallowed fledgling operations in the Caucasus and the Ukraine. Dobrolet was renamed Dobroflot in 1930 and Aeroflot two years later. In the 1930s Antonov and Tupolev

aircraft began to open up air routes across Russia's vast land mass.

The makers of Aeroflot's equipment have striven to mirror the pace of technical development in the west. After the ravages of World War II, the airline restarted operations with the Soviet-built DC-3 clone, the Lisunov Li-2. Later the twin piston-engined Iluyshin Il-14 took up the burden of air operations in the massive country with its developing Siberian region and harsh climatic conditions.

The need to operate from rugged airstrips, sometimes in sub-zero temperatures with minimal support equipment, and the close integration with the military have shaped the rugged style of Aeroflot operations. In the late 1950s Aeroflot stayed in step with the West, introducing the Il-18 and Tu-114 turboprops and the Tu 104 jet airliner. Indeed, when the Tu 104 entered service in September 1956, it was for a few years the world's only jet airliner in service until the later Comets and the Boeing 707 were introduced. The Iluyshin Il-62, still very much in active service, mirrored Britain's VC-10. But the attempt to emulate the Anglo-French Concorde with the Tu-144 SST ended in disaster.

The wide-body revolution inaugurated by the Boeing 747 passed the

Left
Tupolev Tu-154M (1985)

Below
The Antonov AN-72, developed partly in response to a need for STOL
performance in remote locations, has above wing mounted turbo fans to
substantially increase wing lift.

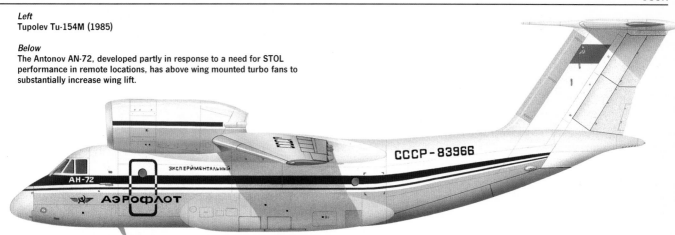

CCCP-83966

ЭКСПЕРИМЕНТАЛЬНЫЙ

АН-72

АЭРОФЛОТ

Soviets by. The four-jet Ilyushin-86 with its twin deck ''walk-on'' baggage hold, again designed for operations from primitive airfields, fell behind western standards of comfort and efficiency.

Aeroflot has struggled hard to catch up, as the internal demand for air travel within the USSR has steadily increased but, as a source of hard currency competing on the world market, the airline was failing to deliver. It was decided therefore to split the giant up into seven new carriers – with a new international operation called ASDA operating western aircraft, including Boeing 747s and 757s, and six regional carriers.

In 1989 the new International Aviation Directorate (IAD) submitted a proposal to the Ministry of Civil Aviation to the effect that it should transform itself into an independent company called Soviet Airlines. A crop of joint venture deals were signed, meanwhile, with western operators such as Lufthansa, Aer Lingus, Marriott and TNT to operate new Airbus A310s, redevelop Moscow's grossly congested Sheremtyevo airport and upgrade customer services and air traffic control.

Early in 1990 Aeroflot signed an agreement to lease five Airbus A310s on its Moscow-London-New York service, beginning in late 1991. Aeroflot executives were also exploring deals to lease or buy Boeing 747-400s, Airbus A330/A340 and McDonnell Douglas MD-11s. The future of the airline now appears bound up with the moves to split the USSR into independant states, many of whom will wish to form their own national airlines. British Airways have recently completed a deal to take a 31% stake in a new airline, Air Russia, which will commence operations in 1994 with seven Boeing 767-300 ERs.

Fleet: 200 international aircraft; 4500 helicopters, domestic and utility types. Passenger aircraft include 194 Antonov An-12, 400 An-24/26/30, eight An-28, three An-72, one An-74; 147 Ilyushin Il-14, 50+ Il-18, 154 Il-62, 72 Il-76, 65+ Il-86; 80+ Let L410/610; 389 Tupolev Tu-134, 369 Tu 154; 750+ Yakovlev Yak 40, 70+ Yak-42-200M. On order 100+ Ilyushin Il-96-300, Il-114, Tu 204, Tu 334, Let L610; five Airbus A310-300. Note: Figures for the Aeroflot fleet are approximate.

Air Canada

The major Canadian airline, state-owned since it was founded in 1937, was privatized in 1989. It carries over 12 million passengers a year and ranks as the world's 17th biggest airline. Canada's international flag carrier was founded as Trans-Canada Airlines, with its shares held by the state-owned Canadian National Railways. Two Lockheed L10As flew the airline's first international route between Vancouver and Seattle, opened in 1938. By the following year transcontinental connections between the eastern and western seaboards had been established. In such a vast country many of its domestic routes were commercially unviable, but were deemed politically and socially necessary. During 1943-47 TCA pilots operated a transatlantic air bridge for mail and key supplies for Canadian armed forces in Europe.

After the war the airline acquired a fleet of war surplus C-47/DC-3s to replace its Lockheeds. The first Canadair-built North Stars (a pressurized, Merlin-powered version of the DC-4) entered service on the North Atlantic in 1947, the airline's growing long-distance services reaching out to the Caribbean and Florida a year later.

In the mid-1950s the fleet consisted of DC-3s and North Stars with Super Constellations now flying the long-haul routes and allowing a Vancouver-Winnipeg- Gander-London service to be introduced. The first turboprops were Vickers Viscounts, introduced in April 1955, and in 1960 the first pure jets, DC-8-50s, went into service between Montreal and Vancouver.

Vickers Vanguard turboprops were introduced in 1961 on the intra-Canadian routes and on services to the cities of the northern US. By

Left
A Boeing 767 showing the latest livery

Above
Boeing 747-100

1963 the last DC-3 had been retired and TCA was all turbine-equipped.

The name was formally changed from TCA to Air Canada in 1965, reflecting the airline's international activities. DC-9s replaced the Viscounts and there was even a short-lived scheme to get aboard the Concorde program. Boeing 747s were introduced on the Toronto-London route in 1971 and Lockheed TriStars on the trans-Canadian routes in 1973.

Today the airline operates an extensive network of scheduled passenger flights within the country, serving Calgary, Charlottestown, Edmonton, Fredericton, Halifax, Moncton, Montreal, Ottawa, Quebec, Regina and Saint John's.

International services are flown to San Francisco, Los Angeles, Chicago, Tampa, Miami, New York, Boston, Freeport, Nassau, Havana, Montego Bay, Kingston, Bermuda, Antigua, St Lucia, Guadeloupe, Martinique, Barbados, Haiti and Puerto Plata, London, Birmingham, Manchester, Paris, Geneva, Zurich, Düsseldorf, Frankfurt, Lisbon, Nice, Vienna and Zagreb.

A group of regional and commuter airlines provide hub and spoke feeder services under the marketing banner Air Canada Connector, and in early 1991 the airline acquired a 100% holding in the Halifax-based Air Nova. In November 1990 the airline had announced the layoff of 2900 personnel and the sale of three Boeing 747-400 on order.

Fleet: seven Airbus A320; three Boeing 747-200B Combi, three 747-100, four Boeing 767-200ER, seven Airbus A320, 17 Boeing 767-200, 26 Boeing 727-200; four Lockheed L-1011-1, four Lockheed L-1011-100, six Lockheed L-10011-500; five McDonnell Douglas DC-8-73F, 35 McDonnell Douglas DC-9-32. On order 27 Airbus A320; nine Boeing 767-300ER

A ir China is the title given to the major sub division the Civil Aviation Administration of China (CAAC) which, prior to 1984, was responsible for all airline operations in mainland China. The CAAC was formed soon after the birth of the People's Republic in 1949. Technical assistance, crew training and aircraft were initially provided by Aeroflot and, up to 1954, Soviet personnel played an important management role in the fledgling airline as it began to spread its routes over this vast nation – with a fleet of Lisunov Li-2s, Ilyushin Il-14s, Il-14Ms and An-2 biplanes. Turboprop Ilyushin Il-18s were introduced on the route from Peking to Irkutsk in 1960. The first non-Soviet type was the Viscount, which entered service in 1964, while in 1970 the first of 39 Hawker Siddeley Tridents were purchased. In the 1970s orders were placed for American aircraft, including ten Boeing 707s and several 747SPs.

Today the huge airline reflects the course of Chinese political development, with many significant aircraft types acquired from the West after the ideological break with the Soviet Union. In 1984 the airline, up to then run as a section of a government department, was broken up to create several regional airlines and the international flag carrier, Air China.

The regional airlines are China East, centered on the port of Shanghai, China Northeast, based on Shenyang, China Northwest at Xian, China Southeast at Guangzhou, and China Southwest at Chengdu. 1986 was a significant year in the airlines overall development when Air China placed a massive order for western airliners, including Boeing 747s, Boeing 767s and Airbus A310s. The same year saw Qantas taking up a contract to provide engineering management, maintenance and crew training for the new fleet. The first entirely home-developed civil air-

Above
A British Aerospace (originally Hawker
Siddeley) Trident 2E

craft, the Xian Y-7 (a Chinese-built version of the Antonov An-24), also went into service, on domestic routes, that year. Since then a nation-wide program of building new airports and upgrading the air traffic control structure of China has been put in hand. In all its regional guises CAAC operates to 261 internal destinations.

Internationally scheduled passenger and freight services are operated to Toronto, San Francisco, Vancouver, New York, Los Angeles, Bucharest, Frankfurt, Paris, Stockholm, Zurich, London, Amsterdam, Rome, Istanbul, Addis Ababa, Belgrade, Sydney Melbourne, Sharjah, Baghdad, Kuwait, Hong Kong, Singapore, Rangoon, Pyongyang, Moscow, Tokyo, Osaka, Nagasaki, Bangkok, Karachi and Manila.

Fleet (All CAAC airlines): three Airbus A300-600ER, three Airbus A310-200, two A310-300; three Boeing 747-400, four Boeing 747SP, one Boeing 747-200F, two 747-200B Combi, one 747-200, five Boeing 757-200, five Boeing 767-200ER, ten Boeing 707-320B/C, 13 Boeing 737-200, three 737-200C, ten 737-300; eight McDonnell Douglas MD-82; ten BAe 146-100. 21 BAe Trident 2E, two Trident 3B; 50+ Antonov An-24; 50+ Ilyushin Il-14, five Ilyushin Il-62, 20+ Ilyushin Il-18; 13+ Tupolev Tu-154M; two Viscounts; 15 Xian Y-7; seven Shorts 360; 12 DHC Twin Otter. On order 5 McDonnell Douglas MD-11, 20 MD-82, five Boeing 747-400, 18 Boeing 757-200, four Boeing 767-200ER, ten Boeing 737-300, five Boeing 737-500; 40 Xian Y-7-100; two Boeing Canada Dash 8-300 (delivered)

Air France

The French national airline, the second biggest in Europe, can trace its origin back to 1933 when the Société Centrale pour l'Exploitation de Lignes Aériennes merged with the smaller Compagnie Générale Aéropostale, under the operating title Air France, and adopted the famous Pegasus badge.

Shortly before the merger the Sociéte had been encouraged by the French government to take over the assets and operations of several smaller airlines which had proliferated in the 1920s, one of which traced its origin back as far as 1919.

In the years before the outbreak of World War II Air France expanded rapidly, with a fleet of over 200 aircraft and flying boats reaching out to Africa, across the Atlantic and to the French colonies in Indo-China. Some routes to North Africa were maintained under Vichy government control during the war, but in 1942 the airline was re-formed in North Africa and operated services based on Algiers, Dakar and Damascus.

Operations were revived in 1946 under the nationalized Société Nationale Air France. In 1948 the operation was merged with Air Bleu (flying airmail) and Air France Transatlantique. Air France's first prestige international route was Paris-New York operated by DC-4s.

The airline once again grew rapidly, building up in the 1950s the world's longest route network and interests in many semi-independent airline operations in France's colonies – interests it kept after their independence. In this period the backbone of the fleet remained DC-3s and DC-4s, with Constellations, Super Constellations and Starliners flying the long-haul routes.

Portly Bréguet Deux Ponts were operated over the Mediterranean until the arrival of the first turboprops, Vickers Viscounts, in 1958 and pure-jet Caravelles and Boeing 707s in 1960. Supersonic services with

Left
Air France was the first airline to put the Airbus A300B2 into service, in May 1974

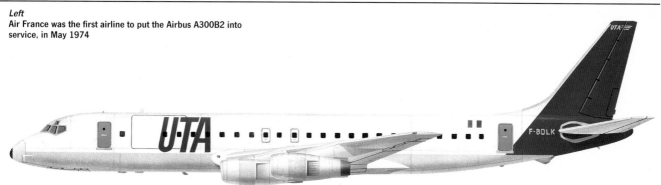

Above
A Douglas DC-8-50 in UTA colors. Air France acquired a controlling interest in 1989

Air France's fleet of seven Concorde SSTs were inaugurated in 1976 from Paris to New York and to South America.

In November 1990 the European Commission cleared Air France's takeover of Air Inter and UTA (Union de Transports Aériens), giving the state-owned flag carrier its own near monopoly on the domestic route network – and access to many more French international routes – in return for giving up eight domestic and 50 international routes to independent and foreign carriers. In 1991 the operations were in the process of merging. The airline was compelled to sell its share of TAT.

UTA itself had been formed in 1963 by the merger of Union Aéromaritime de Transport (UAT) and Compagnie de Transports Aériens Intercontinentaux. UTA had considerable shareholdings in Air Inter, The French domestic operator, and Sodetraf, the holding company for Air Afrique. It has other interests in airport services, hotels and holiday villages in Polynesia and New Caledonia.

UTA operates flights from Paris (Charles de Gaulle), Nice, Marseilles, Lyon and Toulouse to 23 points in Africa, to Bahrain and Muscat, Los Angeles, San Francisco, Honolulu and Tokyo, and to eight other destinations in the Pacific area.

Fleet (Air France): seven Aérospatiale/BAe Concorde; 20 Boeing 727-200, 16 Boeing 737-200, 16 Boeing 747-100, two 747-200B, 11 Boeing 747-200M Combi, eight 747-200F; One 747-400, 15 Airbus A300B2/B4, seven Airbus A310-200, three A310-300, 14 Airbus A320, one C160 Transall. On order 15 Boeing 747-400, five 747-400F, two 747-200F; two Airbus A310-300, 11 Airbus A320, seven Airbus A340-300, 12 Boeing 757-500, One Boeing 747-200F, 19 Boeing 747-400. NOTE: Figures do not include Air Inter aircraft

Fleet (UTA): one Boeing 747-400, one 747-300 Combi, two 747-200F; six McDonnell Douglas DC-10-30. On order one Boeing 747-400; six Airbus A340-300

Air India

The international airline and national flag carrier of India was founded in 1946. It succeeded Tata Airlines, which had been founded in 1932 when operations began with a de Havilland Puss Moth flying a five-hop route from Karachi to Madras. Carrying mail was the airline's primary business before the outbreak of war – taking it by air in a fleet of DH86s and DH89s all over the sub-continent after it had arrived from Britain by Imperial Airways flying boat.

At the end of World War II, in the face of competition from small bush airlines springing up all over India with cheap and abundant surplus aircraft, Tata Airlines re-formed and relaunched itself in 1946 under the name Air India Ltd, with a fleet of DC-3s, DC-4s and newly ordered Vick-

ers Vikings. TWA gave technical assistance.

In 1947 the Indian government took a minority shareholding in the company and a year later a Lockheed Constellation inaugurated the airline's first international route – to London from Bombay via Cairo and Geneva. The airline was restyled Air India International Ltd.

In 1953 the airline was fully nationalized, with sole rights to fly international traffic. Seven smaller operators were meanwhile amalgamated to form the domestic carrier, Indian Airlines.

As the state airline pushed its route network out further, it acquired a fleet of nine Lockeed Super Constellations operated in conjunction with BOAC and Qantas on a route from New York to Sydney via London and

Left
A Boeing 747 sporting brand-new livery

Bombay. A service from Bombay to Moscow was opened in 1959 and a year later the airline began to operate its first jets – Boeing 707s. In 1962 it adopted its present title – Air India. The first Boeing 747s were delivered in 1971 for use on routes to London and New York.

At the end of 1990 Air India drew up its new fleet blueprint with a requirement for 12 new long-range airliners, either Airbus A340s, McDonnell Douglas MD-11s or Boeing 777s, and turned its Boeing 747-400 options into firm orders.

Air India flies scheduled passenger services from Bombay, Delhi, Calcutta, Trivandrum, Hyderabad, Goa and Madras to points in the Far and Middle East, North America, Europe, Africa and Australia.

Fleet: three Airbus A300B4, eight Airbus A310-300; two Boeing 747-300 Combi, nine 747-200B. Leased; one Il-76, one Il-62, one Boeing 747F. On order four 747-400

Above
An Airbus A310-300. The type entered service in late 1985

Air New Zealand

Formed in 1939 as Tasman Empire Airlines (or TEAL), New Zealand's flag carrier originally had major shareholders from Australia and Britain. The airline's primary role was to provide an air link across the Tasman Sea to Australia – using two Short S23 flying boats on the Auckland to Sydney route three times a week.

In 1946 Short Sandringham flying boats started service on the route but repeated technical problems led to their being withdrawn and replaced by four Mk IV Solents. In the meantime DC-4s were temporarily chartered from TAA. Three DC-6s were taken into the fleet following the break-up of British Commonwealth Pacific Airlines in 1953 and used to inaugurate an Auckland-Melbourne service. Short Solent flying boats remained operational on this route until 1960. In 1959 Lockheed Electras replaced the DC-6s.

In 1961 the national government acquired full control. The current name was adopted in 1965, the year the first pure-jets, Douglas DC-8-52s, went into service. A dramatic route expansion followed, with authority granted to fly to Los Angeles, Singapore and Hong Kong. The first wide-bodies, DC-10-30s, went into service in 1973. The crash of an Air New Zealand DC-10 on a sight-seeing trip over Antarctica in 1979 was a major commercial blow for the airline, also causing considerable damage to its morale. It moved to replace the Douglas tri-jets with Boeing 747s. The first 747-400 series went into service on the Auckland-Los Angeles route in November 1990.

In 1978 the state-owned domestic airline New Zealand National Airways Corporation, with its fleet of Viscounts and F27s, was merged with the international operation.

Fleet: two Boeing 747-400, five Boeing 747-200B, eight Boeing 767-200ER, 11 Boeing 737-200. On order six Boeing 737-300, one Boeing 747-400, two Boeing 767-300. NOTE: 15 Fokker F27s were withdrawn from service and put up for sale.

Alitalia

The national airline of Italy was refounded soon after World War II with capital assistance from Britain and began flying operations in 1947. Ten years later it merged with Linee Aeree Italiane or LAI (40% owned by Trans World Airways) to become the single Italian domestic and international operator.

The airline's early postwar equipment consisted of Fiat G12s and Savoia Marchetti SM95s plus two Lancastrians – civilianized bombers which were ambitiously put to work on a service to South America in

continued

1948. In 1949 DC4s were acquired to fly the international routes, together with a fleet of DC-3s for domestic work and to service a growing schedule of operations to North Africa, the Middle East and the cities of western Europe. Convair C340s, 440s, DC-6Bs and DC-7Cs arrived in the mid-1950s, turboprop Viscounts in 1956 and the first pure jets, Sud Caravelle IIIs and Douglas DC-8s, in 1960-61 to service an ever-expanding route network. Wide-body operations began with the first Boeing 747-143 in 1970, while DC-10-30s were acquired in 1973.

The airline has recently had a turbulent commercial history and underwent a major structural reorganization in 1987, which has returned it to profit after a period of heavy losses. The Italian state, with a stake of 83.4%, is the major shareholder.

Naples-based Aero Trasporti Italiani (ATI) is a wholly owned subsidiary operating an extensive domestic network within Italy and to Sardinia. Today Alitalia itself flies both an extensive domestic and a global network of scheduled passenger services from its chief hubs of Milan and Rome to the major cities of Europe, the Americas, Africa, the Middle and Far East and Australia

Page 45
Airbus A300

Above
McDonnell Douglas DC-9

Fleet: 14 Airbus A300B4; five Boeing 747-200B Combi, one 747-200F, six 747-200B; 43 McDonnell Douglas DC-9-30, 28 McDonnell Douglas MD-82, 11 ATR-42. On order 40 Airbus A321; six McDonnell Douglas MD-11 Combi; 15 McDonnell Douglas MD-82, 25 MD-87
Fleet (ATI): nine ATR 42; 17 McDonnell Douglas DC-9-30; 12 McDonnell Douglas MD-82

One of three major Japanese airlines, ANA was originally formed in 1952 as Japan Helicopter and Aeroplane Transport Company (JHAT) and was intended to specialise in Japan's domestic routes leaving Japan Airlines to develop international services. JHAT merged with Far Eastern Airlines in 1958 when the present title was adopted and subsequently took over Fujita Airlines in 1963, Nakanihon Air Services in 1965, and Nagasaki Airways in 1967. In 1971 ANA began to operate international charter flights but a more significant milestone occurred in 1986 when, following a change in government policy, ANA was permitted to operate international scheduled services. Beginning with a route to Guam from Tokyo, the route network was quickly expanded to include Los Angeles, Beijing, Hong

continued

Kong, Seoul and Sydney while today London, Moscow, Vienna, Bangkok, Saipan and Stockholm are also served. New routes for 1991 include Nagoya-Honolulu, Fukuoka-Bangkok, Hiroshima-Seoul, Narita-Berlin and Narita-New York.

Despite this expansion, ANA still maintains a comprehensive domestic and regional network connecting over 70 destinations. Many of these routes are operated by Air Nippon, a wholly owned subsidiary operating a small fleet of Boeing 737s and NAMC YS-11s and which carried over 2.5 million passengers in 1990. Parent ANA carried no less than 30 million in the same period and the combined total makes it the world's busiest airline outside the United States. ANA employs over 13,000 staff and has placed great emphasis on service to customer, winning the prestigious Air Transport World award in this category in 1990. As part of a constant policy to maintain a modern aircraft fleet the airline was the second customer for Boeing's new 777, placing orders for 15 aircraft at the end of 1990.

Page 47
Boeing 747-200

Above
Lockheed Tristar

Fleet: Five Airbus A320, two Boeing 747-400, seventeen 7747SR, five 747-200, nineteen 767-300, twenty-five 767-200, fourteen 737-200, eleven Lockheed Tristar, twelve NAMC YS-11A. On order (excluding options): Five Airbus A340, eight Airbus 320, twenty-one Boeing 747-400, five 767-300, fifteen 777.

American Airlines

Texas-based American Airlines has grown into one of the world's most significant air transport operations. It was founded in 1934 as the successor to American Airways. This had been formed four years earlier to fly the southern transcontinental air mail route generously awarded by the US postmaster general, having already in 1929 taken over several smaller airlines under its previous name, Aviation Corporation. Soon passengers were being carried by American Airlines and the big biplane, Curtiss Condor, was introduced, with sleeping berths and an in-flight stewardess to tend travelers as they fitfully slumbered between multiple stops.

The first DC-3 went into service in June 1936, flying Chicago-New York. In its flamboyant livery, the modernity of the new airliner, plus its comfort and efficiency, were the focus of an aggressive marketing effort. In common with other US airlines, much of American's fleet was called up for war service during 1942-5. In 1945 American merged with American Export Airlines to form American Overseas Airlines, fly-

ing a marginally profitable service from New York to London with DC-4s. In 1950 the operation was sold to Pan American.

American got its first postwar-built equipment, the Douglas DC-6s, into service in 1947 and began a major program that would eclipse its competitors. The DC-4s were retired by 1948, the DC-3s a year later, to be replaced by Convair CV240 twinprops. The turboprop Lockheed Electra went into service in January 1959, followed a few days later by the first Boeing 707 – flying non-stop from New York to Los Angeles. The new jet gave American a tremendous edge over its rival United, still waiting for delivery of its first DC-8s and meanwhile having to plug away with piston power over its transcontinental routes. American put turbofan-powered Boeing 720Bs into service in 1961 and the flamboyant but commercially unsuccessful Convair CV990 Coronado in 1962.

Boeing 727s began to replace the DC-6s and DC-7s now flying American's regional feeder routes, until the airline's last piston-powered flight was made on 17 December 1966. As the wide-body era

loomed, American ordered the Boeing 747 off the drawing board in 1967 and was a launch customer for the Douglas DC-10 in 1969.

In 1986 American took over the California-based Air Cal, giving the carrier an extensive route network along the US west coast. Today American's US-wide domestic network operates from five main hubs at Chicago, Dallas, Nashville, Raleigh/Durham and San Juan. A sixth hub, at San José, was due to come on stream in 1991. American's parent organization, AMR, also controls a number of regional and commuter airlines which feed passengers into the AA hubs under the marketing banner "American Eagle", operating a combined fleet of 211 twin turboprops.

Transatlantic scheduled passenger services are flown to London, Brussels, Düsseldorf, Frankfurt, Geneva, Hamburg, Lyon, Madrid, Manchester, Munich, Paris, Stockholm and Zurich. Operations across the Pacific from Dallas to Tokyo commenced in 1987. Other points are served in the Caribbean, Canada and Mexico. In early 1991 American

Page 49
British Aerospace 146-200
Left: An Airbus A300-600, at Miami
Above: A British Aerospace Jetstream 31, operating under the "American Eagle" commuter network banner.

was negotiating to take over TWA's Heathrow services. McDonnell Douglas MD-11 services to Tokyo began in March 1991.

Fleet: 25 Airbus A300-600R; two Boeing 747SP, 34 Boeing 757-200, 15 Boeing 767-300ER, 22 767-200ER, eight 767-200, five Boeing 737-300, ten 737-200, 125 Boeing 727-200, 39 727-100; six BAe 146-200; 2 McDonnell Douglas MD-11, ten DC-10-30, 49 DC-10-10, 225 McDonnell Douglas MD-80. On order ten Airbus A300-600R; 55 Boeing 757-200, 21 Boeing 767-300ER; 75 Fokker 100; 17 McDonnell Douglas MD-11, 35 McDonnell Douglas MD-80

British Airways

The biggest airline in Europe is also one of its oldest. Through a multiplicity of precursor companies, BA has an exotic and complex pedigree. In August 1919 the Air Transport and Travel Company flew the world's first scheduled civil airline international flight – from London to Paris. A DH4A bomber, with its rear fuselage converted into a primitive cabin, carried a single passenger and a crate of letters and cargo from capital to capital in two and a half hours. A month later a rival sprang up, the Handley Page company, famous for its World War I bomber designs, flying one of its 0/400 bombers from Cricklewood, north London, also to Paris. A third operator on the London-Paris route, Instone Airlines, began operations in 1920.

The pioneers found great difficulties in making their operations profitable, in spite of British government subsidies introduced in 1921 as part of a plan to nurture civil aviation. Government and commercial pressure shunted the three airlines together, along with a fourth, British Marine Air Navigation. In April 1924 Imperial Airways, as the new carrier was dubbed, made its first flight from London to Paris. With the vast span of the British empire as its market and a government-granted monopoly of international operations, Imperial Airways began to reach out to India, the Far East and Australia, using both landplanes and increasingly sophisticated and luxurious flying boats. A through route to India was opened in 1929 and by 1933 it had reached Singapore where Qantas Empire Airways picked up the connection to Brisbane. In July 1937 flying boats began a transatlantic service from Southampton to New York. The Empire Air Mail scheme of 1938, which underwrote a flat fee air mail price throughout the British colonies, boosted the air-

Above left
Lockheed L-1011-200

Above
A Rolls-Royce powered version of the latest 400 series Boeing 747

continued

line's revenue.

In spite of Imperial's international monoply granted in the original agreement of 1924, in 1936 a challenger sprang up on the European routes. British Airways flew from Heston airfield in west London to Paris and other European capitals, with a fleet of DH86s, Fokkers, Junkers and Lockheed L.10s. On 1 April 1940, with Britain at war on the eve of the German offensive in the west, the British Overseas Airways Corporation (BOAC) was created, under state sponsorship. It had a fleet of 82 aircraft.

In the face of enemy action throughout the war BOAC maintained services to the outposts of Empire and across the Atlantic (using Boeing 314 flying boats). The airline emerged into the postwar world with a huge route network and a rag-bag of worn-out aircraft. There were only converted bombers like the Avro Lancastrian and Handley-Page Halton to take up the burden. The new Labour government set about reorganizing Britain's nationalized air transport industry. British South American Airways (BSAA) was established to operate services across the South Atlantic, but much more significant was the creation of British European Airways (BEA) in 1946 to fly the flag in Europe.

Soon new aircraft rather than converted bombers began to join BOAC's fleet – Constellations to fly London-New York in 1946 and Canadair built DC-4s (known by BOAC as Argonauts), plus Boeing Stratocruisers in 1949. That year BSAA was merged with BOAC after a series of crashes had grounded its fleet of Avro Tudors. BEA swallowed up a number of smaller operators after the war, flying its growing fleet of DC-3s, Vikings and DH89s to an increasing number of destinations in and around the British Isles and to an equally expanding number of European capitals. BEA played an important role during the 1948 Berlin airlift.

On 2 May 1952 the revolutionary de Havilland Comet jet airliner went into service on BOAC's London-Johannesburg route, heralding what should have been a tremendous technical and commercial break-through for the loss-making airline – the first to offer civil jet transport. However, two tragic Comet crashes over the Mediterranean in 1954 grounded the fleet and dashed BOAC's and the British aircraft industry's hopes of seizing the lead from the Americans. Turboprop Bristol Britannias went into service on the African routes in 1955. The longer-range Britannia 312 began to span the Atlantic in 1957, supplanting Constellations and Douglas DC-7Cs. The redesigned Comet 4C began the first pure-jet transatlantic service in October 1958 (narrowly beating Pan Am who started services with the Boeing 707 a few days later), but the Corporation's management had already placed orders for the aircraft that was truly to be the harbinger of mass jet air travel – the Boeing 707. Powered by Rolls-Royce Conway turbofan engines, the 707s entered service on BOAC's North Atlantic routes in 1960, as the Comets were switched to the Far East and Australia.

BEA's postwar fleet, still largely made up of DC-3s (dubbed ''Pionairs'' by the airline) was augmented in 1952 by the introduction of the Airspeed Ambassador (named Elizabethan Class by the airline) and the first turboprop Viscount in 1953. Medium-range Comet 4Bs furnished the airline's first pure-jets in 1958. Vanguard turboprops and Trident trijets (the first aircraft certificated for fully automated landings) followed in the early 1960s together with a fleet of BAe One-Elevens mostly committed to the airline's intra-West German route network. This was a hangover from the war, but it proved an important commercial operation for BEA and its successor, British Airways, until Germany regained the right to operate internal air services in 1990.

In the early 1960s Vickers VC-10s and Super VC-10s joined the BOAC fleet at the same time, during a period when the airline was struggling to make a profit as it contemplated a leap into a new era of air travel with the development of the Anglo-French Concorde SST (supersonic transport). This technological marvel was on the margins of commercial practicality, and meanwhile US industry had stolen a march on Britain and Europe with the development of the wide-body generation of airliners. In 1968 BOAC ordered its first Boeing 747s, while BEA

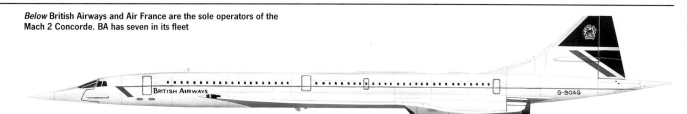

Below British Airways and Air France are the sole operators of the Mach 2 Concorde. BA has seven in its fleet

Below
BEA started operations with Vickers-Armstrong Vikings in 1946

opted for the Lockheed TriStar.

In 1969 a British government inquiry recommended the merger of the two operations. The new British Airways was formed in 1972 and began formally integrated operations on 1 April 1974. The airline made history in 1976 when, along with Air France, it began regular supersonic scheduled passenger services with Concorde. In April 1977 the airline was further rationalized into a single unified operating structure, with an aggressive marketing strategy looking for worldwide business.

In February 1987 the state-owned airline was privatized and within ten months had swallowed up British Caledonian, the major independent British carrier. BA's charter operation, British Airtours, was renamed Caledonian Airways in 1989. In 1990 BA conceived an ambitious plan to develop a new European hub at Brussels, with a shareholding in a new operation called Sabena World Airways (SWA), in partnership with the Belgian flag carrier and KLM. Fuel price rises and the airline recession caused the scheme to be temporarily shelved early in 1991.

British Airways flies scheduled passenger services to over 170 destinations in 77 countries in Europe, the Near, Middle and Far East, the Caribbean and the Americas. The airline's domestic operations link 15 points in the UK and include the high-frequency "super shuttle" service between London, (Heathrow) and Glasgow, Edinburgh, Manchester and Belfast. All routes to Ireland were abandoned in 1991 as part of a rationalization program to combat recession in the industry.

Fleet: seven Aérospatiale/BAe Concorde; ten Airbus A320; seven Boeing 747-400, 18 747-200B, six 747-200 Combi, 16 747-100, nine Boeing 767-300, 36 Boeing 757-200, 44 Boeing 737-200, four 737-300; 30 BAe One-Eleven-500; eight BAe ATP; eight BAe 748; nine Lockheed L-1011-1, eight L-1011-200; eight McDonnell Douglas DC-10-30. On order: 15 Boeing 777, 23 Boeing 747-400, eight Boeing 767-300, five Boeing 757-200, 24 Boeing 737-300, five BAe ATP. NOTE: BAe ATPs and 748s are operated by BA's Glasgow-based Highland Division

Canadian
CANADIAN AIRLINES INTERNATIONAL

This airline, formed at the outset of 1988, is heir to a famous name in transport history – Canadian Pacific. What was then the second largest airline in Canada was merged with the major regional carrier, Pacific Western Airlines, to form the new, Calgary-based operation. It is owned by PWA Corporation, which has a large base of small private shareholders.

Canadian Pacific was formed in 1942 as an amalgam of ten small operators and international services began in 1949 when Canadair 4s, Merlin-engined versions of the Douglas DC-4, opened a route from Vancouver to Sydney, via San Francisco, Honolulu, Canton Island and Fiji. Scheduled services to Amsterdam began using DC-6Bs, in 1955. Bristol Britannia 314/324s began non-stop transcontinental flights within the country in 1959. The first pure-jets, Douglas DC-8s, were ordered in 1961, eventually replacing the Britannias and DC-6s on international routes.

The airline grew rapidly in the 1980s, swallowing up Eastern Provincial Airways and its affiliate, Air Maritime and Nordair. It took over

Above
A McDonnell Douglas DC-10-30 in the new CAI livery, modified from that of Canadian Pacific

Quebecair in 1986, and acquired a stake in Air Atlantic.

Today the airline flies an extensive domestic route network to 90 destinations in Canada and the northern US, its hubs being fed by commuter airlines operating under the Canadian Partner marketing alliance.

Internationally the airline flies to 86 destinations in over 20 countries with scheduled passenger and freight services offered to Amsterdam, Milan, Buenos Aires, Lima, Rio de Janeiro, Santiago, São Paulo, Bangkok, Beijing, Hong Kong, Shanghai, Tokyo, Auckland, Sydney, Nadi, Honolulu, Los Angeles and San Francisco.

Fleet: 10 Airbus A310-300, 5 A320, 52 Boeing 737-200, 2 Boeing 747-100, 12 Boeing 767-300ER; 8 McDonnell Douglas DC-10-30. On order 6 Boeing 767-300ER, six Boeing 747-400, 17 Airbus A320-200

Cathay Pacific

Above
A Boeing 747-200 on its final approach to Hong Kong

This international airline centered on Hong Kong was started in 1946 by two air force cargo-pilots, veterans of flying the "hump" air bridge from India to China. They set up a cargo airline with a couple of war-weary DC-3s, flying from Sydney to Shanghai. In 1948 the Swire trading group acquired a 45% stake and its headquarters were shifted to Hong Kong.

A small fleet of DC-3s and Catalina amphibians began to fly a regional air network from the crown colony, pushing out to new destinations as longer-legged types joined the fleet — DC-6s and DC-6Bs in the early 1950s, then turboprop Lockheed Electras in 1959, the year Cathay absorbed its rival, Hong Kong Airlines. The first pure-jets, Convair CV 880s, were ordered in 1960.

Skilful management and marketing and the booming economy of the region have seen Cathay Pacific grow into a major world airline. Swire Pacific retains a controlling shareholding; the rest is owned by the Hong Kong and Shanghai Banking Corporation, and the China International Trust and Investment Corporation.

Scheduled passenger and freight services are operated to Abu Dhabi, Amsterdam, Auckland, Bahrain, Bangkok, Beijing, Bombay, Brisbane, Brunei, Denpasar, Dubai, Frankfurt, Fukuoka, Jakarta, Kaoshing, Kota Kinabalu, Kuala Lumpur, London, Manila, Manchester, Mauritius, Melbourne, Nagoya, Osaka, Paris, Penang, Perth, Port Moresby, Rome, San Francisco, Seoul, Shanghai, Singapore, Sydney, Taipei, Tokyo, Vancouver and Zurich.

Fleet: nine Boeing 747-400, six Boeing 747-300, eight 747-200, three 747-200F; 18 Lockheed TriStar. On order ten Airbus A330-300; nine Boeing 747-400, two 747-400F

Continental

Houston-based Continental Airlines, the fourth largest US carrier at the end of the 1980s, went into Chapter 11 bankruptcy protection at the end of 1990, blaming its plight on the effect of the Gulf crisis on rising fuel costs. Seven years earlier it had gone through a similar crisis but had survived.

The airline traces it roots back to July 1934 when it began operations as Varney Speed Lines. In 1937 Varney bought the Denver-Pueblo route of Wyoming Air Service, moved to Denver and changed its name to Continental. The merger with Pioneer Airlines and the granting of the Chicago – Los Angeles route via Denver in 1955 marked its transition from a regional airline to a mainline operation with a fleet of DC-7Bs, DC-6Bs and DC-3s. Viscounts appeared in 1958 and Boeing 707-124s in 1960.

In 1981 Texas Air bought a controlling interest and merged the airline with its own Texas International (formed orginally in 1940 as Aviation Enterprises). In September 1983 Continental filed for Chapter 11 protection, slashing its domestic route network from 78 points to 25 and its workforce by two-thirds.

The airline clambered back into profit and in 1987 the operations of the People Express Group (Frontier, People Express, Britt Airways and Provincetown Boston Airlines) and New York Air were merged into Continental, doubling its size. In 1988 Continental struck a deal with SAS to co-ordinate marketing, flight codes and scheduling. In 1990 Continental operated to 82 US domestic and 42 international destinations from its four major hubs at Denver, Houston, Newark and Cleveland, fed by a web of feeder services under the name Continental Express.

Three of the feeder operators, Britt, Bar Harbor and Rocky Mountain, are in turn Texas Air subsidiaries. As its cash crisis deepened in 1990 Continental sold its Seattle – Tokyo route authority to American Airlines but talks with Delta on other Pacific routes were not concluded.

Fleet: 17 Airbus A300B4; six Boeing 747-200, two Boeing 747-100, 95 Boeing 727-100/200, 94 Boeing 737-100/200/300; eight McDonnell

Above left
A Boeing 737-300

Above
A Boeing 747-100

Douglas DC-10-30, seven DC-10-10, 31 McDonnell Douglas DC-9-30, 65 McDonnell Douglas MD-80. On order 20 Airbus A330/340, 50 Boeing 737-300, 25 Boeing 757-200.

Atlanta-based Delta absorbed Western Airlines in 1987 to become the third largest carrier in the US. The giant can trace its origin to a Louisiana-based crop duster, founded in 1924, working in the cotton fields of the Mississippi delta – hence the name. The company entered the passenger business in June 1929 with the Beech Travelairs flying from Atlanta to Dallas via Jackson, Mississippi. Delta was frozen out of the notorious US Air Mail contract hand-outs of 1930 and had to struggle on until 1934 when the Roosevelt administration reviewed the mail monopolies. After the US Army tried briefly to fly the mails, Delta was awarded a mail route, from Charleston to Fort Worth, flown at first with a Stinson T, later a Stinson A. An increase in passenger traffic led the airline to acquire Lockheed Electras, then DC-3s (in 1940), as its route network and traffic volume expanded.

In 1941 the new Civil Aeronautics Board (CAB) awarded a clutch of new routes to Delta with its new fast-growing hub at Atlanta. The outbreak of war meant that the airline's Electras and DC-3s were im-pressed for transport duty and its maintenance and crew-training facilities turned over to war work.

After the war Delta picked up again with a fleet of war-surplus DC-3s and DC-4s, introducing an inclusive tour operation to Florida to fill seats after the 1947 slump in US air travel. Boom times returned in the 1950s when Delta began a period of rapid expansion through take-overs. The airline's splendid Detroit-inspired livery now adorned the Constellations of Chicago and Southern Airlines, taken over in 1953. Later in the decade, Convair CV340s, 440s and DC-7s were the last piston-powered airliners to enter the fleet. In 1962 DC-8s arrived, to be followed by Convair CV880s in 1960 and DC-9s in 1966.

In 1972 Delta took over Northeast Airlines, the successor to Boston and Maine Airways (founded in 1933), inheriting a fleet of 727s, DC-9s and FH-227 US-built twinprop Friendships. The big leap for Delta came in 1987 when it took over Western Airlines. Western traced its origin to the Western Air Transport Company founded in 1925 as an air mail car-

rier operating from Salt Lake City to Los Angeles. Part of the company was split off to form TWA. The rest was briefly owned by General Motors who sold the operation on in 1934 to a Pennsylvania coal-owner who shunted the airline into a joint operating deal with United.

Postwar the company prospered modestly. Western had an off-on flirtation with Continental in the 1970s, but a bid for growth after deregulation left it sorely depleted of cash and ripe for takeover by Delta.

Today the airline offers scheduled passenger services to Acapulco, Calgary, Dublin, Edmonton, Frankfurt, Guadalajara, Hamilton, Hamburg, Ixtapa, Juarez, London, Mazatlan, Mexico City, Montreal, Munich, Nassau, Paris, Puerto Vallarta, Seoul, Shannon, Stuttgart, Taipei, Tokyo and Vancouver.

An extensive feeder network is operated under the Delta Connection banner involving Cincinnati-based Comair, Boston-New York-based Business Express, Atlanta-based Atlantic Southwest and Salt Lake City-Los Angeles-based Skywest.

Above left
Boeing 767-300

Above
Delta currently operate a fleet of 22 Lockheed L-1011-1 TriStars.

Fleet: three McDonnell Douglas DC-10-10, five McDonnell Douglas DC-8-71, ten TriStar 500, one TriStar 200, six TriStar 250, 22 TriStar 1, 16 Boeing 767-300, six Boeing 767-300ER, 15 Boeing 767-200, 61 Boeing 757-200, 129 Boeing 727-200, 13 Boeing 737-300, 59 Boeing 737-200, two McDonnell Douglas MD-11, 67 McDonnell-Douglas MD-88, 36 McDonnell-Douglas DC-9-32; On Order; five Airbus A330, seven A340, 19 757-200, 57 737-300, 38 MD-88, six 767-300ER, 14 767-300, 11 MD-11, 50 MD-90

EgyptAir

The national airline of Egypt traces its origin to Misr Airwork, founded in Cairo in 1932. In 1949 the now wholly Egyptian-owned operation was renamed Misrair. This was merged with Syrian Airlines during 1960-63 in the short lived United Arab Airlines which flew Comet 4Cs, Viscounts and DC-3s over a regional Middle East route network centered on Cairo, Alexandria and Damascus. The Boeing 707s were delivered in 1968. The company was renamed Egyptair in 1971 and today is owned by the state bank of Egypt and the Misr insurance company.

Scheduled international passenger and freight services serve Athens, Barcelona, Brussels, Copenhagen, Düsseldorf, Frankfurt, Geneva, Helsinki, Istanbul, Larnaca, London, Madrid, Milan, Munich, Paris, Rome, Stockholm, Vienna, Zurich, Abu Dhabi, Amman, Bahrain, Damascus, Dharan, Doha, Dubai, Riyadh, Jeddah, Kuwait, Muscat, Ras Al Khaimah, Sana'a, Sharjah, Algiers, Abidjan, Accra, Benghazi, Dar-es-Salaam, Kano, Khartoum, Lagos, Nairobi, Tripoli and Tunis, Bangkok, Bombay, Karachi, Manchester, Tokyo, Los Angeles and New York.

Fleet: nine Airbus A300-600, six Airbus A300B4, four Airbus A320; six Boeing 707-366, seven Boeing 737-200, two Boeing 747-300 Combi, three Boeing 767-200ER, two Boeing 767-300ER; two Fokker F.27, one Lockheed TriStar. On order; three Airbus A300-600R, seven Airbus A320, 5 Boeing 737-500

Above left
A Boeing 737-200 at Abu Simbel

Above
An Airbus A300 at London, Heathrow

Below
The short-to-medium-range Airbus Industrie A300 first entered
service in 1974

El Al ISRAEL AIRLINES

A national airline was set up soon after the foundation of the new state of Israel in 1948. The state-owned El Al began services to Europe in 1949 using DC-4s and to the US and South Africa a year later using Lockheed Constellations.

Britannias were acquired in 1957 and the first jets, Boeing 707s, in 1961. Because of the exigencies of Middle East politics, El Al has long rehearsed very stringent anti-terrorist regimes and its aircraft are fitted with anti-missile electronic devices.

El Al was the first airline to use the twin engined Boeing 767 on transatlantic flights when it started an 11 hour non stop scheduled service from Montreal to Tel Aviv in 1984. At that time the aircraft had to operate within the 60 minute rule (i.e. always within one hours flying time of a suitable diversion airfield) but El Al's experience was instrumental in obtaining EROPS clearance for this and other modern twinjets.

Scheduled passenger and freight services are operated from Tel Aviv to Amsterdam, Athens, Brussels, Bucharest, Budapest, Cairo, Cologne, Copenhagen, Frankfurt, Geneva, London, Manchester, Marseilles, Lisbon, Madrid, Istanbul, Munich, Paris, Rome, Vienna, Warsaw, Zagreb, Zurich, Nairobi, Johannesburg, New York, Toronto,

Montreal, Miami, Chicago, Los Angeles, and Boston. There is also a service from the resort of Eilat to London.

Fleet: five Boeing 747-200B, two Boeing 747-200B Combi, one Boeing 747-200F, one 747-100F, two Boeing 767-200, two 767-200ER, five Boeing 757-200, two 707, two 737-200. On order: two Boeing 747-400.

Above left
A Boeing 747
Below left
The Lockheed Constellation started airline service with El Al in
1950

Above
El Al operates both 100 and 200 series Boeing 747s

The flag-carrier of Indonesia was established in colonial days when in 1950 the local Indonesian government and the Dutch airline KLM formed a new company as a successor to the Inter-Island Division of the Dutch airline, which in turn had succeeded the prewar KNILM – Royal Netherlands East Indies Airlines.

Domestic service across the huge pattern of islands that make up the Asian country began with a fleet of DC-3s and Catalinas. In 1958 the recently independent Indonesian state nationalized the operation with a route network now pushed out to to Manila, Bangkok and Singapore. The first turboprops, Lockheed Electras, entered service in 1961.

In 1963 Guruda took over the operations of the Dutch managed De Kroonduif company, at the time flying a fleet of DC-3s, Beavers and Twin Pioneers in West New Guinea. A year later these operations were passed to Merpati Nusantara, the domestic operator – itself taken over by Garuda in 1978 – but continuing to trade to date under its original name. Merpati has recently ordered five BAe ATPs for use on inter-island services.

Today Garuda flies scheduled passenger and freight services from Jakarta to London, Amsterdam, Frankfurt, Paris, Vienna, Zurich, Cairo, Abu Dhabi, Jeddah, Riyadh, Bangkok, Kuala Lumpur, Singapore, Honolulu, Hong Kong, Manila, Taipei, Saigon, Seoul, Sydney, Perth, Melbourne, Darwin, Port Headland, Auckland, Honolulu, Los Angeles and Tokyo.

Fleet: six Boeing 747-200, two Boeing 737-300; six McDonnell Douglas DC-10-30, nine Airbus A300B4, 18 McDonnell Douglas DC-9-32; six Fokker F28-2000, 28 F28-4000. On order, 9 Airbus A330-300, 16 Boeing 737-300, 9 Boeing 747-400, 6 McDonnell Douglas MD-11, 12 Fokker 100.

Gulf Air

Above
A Lockheed L-1011 at London, Heathrow

Set up in 1950 as Gulf Aviation Company Ltd, based on the island of Bahrain, but wholly owned and managed by British Overseas Airways Corporation, Gulf Air has grown along with the economic importance of the region. In its early days it flew two DC-3s, four DH Herons and three Doves around the Gulf and the Arabian Peninsula.

Since 1974 all the shares in the airline have been owned by the Gulf states of Bahrain, Oman, Qatar and the United Arab Emirates. In 1985 the UAE withdrew to set up its own official carrier, Emirates Airlines.

At the end of 1990 Gulf ordered 12 new Boeing 767-300ERs to operate its new Sydney-Singapore service. The airline is also considering expansion of its Far East routes including flights to Korea, Peking and Hong Kong and expansion in this direction will require purchase of aircraft such as the MD-11 or Airbus A330/340. Gulf air carries out all maintenance work on its 737 fleet, except for the engines which are serviced by Sabena, and claims the world's best technical dispatch regularity for these aircraft.

The international routes served are from Bahrain to Abu Dhabi, Al Fujairah, Amman, Athens, Baghdad, Bangkok, Bombay, Cairo, Colombo, Dhaka, Damascus, Dar-es-Salaam, Dharan, Delhi, Doha, Dubai, Frankfurt, Hong Kong, Istanbul, Jeddah, Karachi, Khartoum, Larnaca, London, Muscat, Manila, Nairobi, New York, Paris, Ras Al Khaima, Riyadh, Salalh, Sana'a and Sharjah.

Fleet: Eight TriStar 200, 11 Boeing 767-300ER, ten Boeing 737-200; On order seven Boeing 767-300ERs, 12 Airbus A320-200.

Iberia LÍNEAS AÉREAS DE ESPAÑA

The national carrier of Spain can trace its origins back to 1921 when the first civil air operations began in the country. In 1925 the airline Unión Aérea Española was founded, and in 1927 a rival calling itself "Iberia" began to trade, offering a service between Madrid and Barcelona using a ten-seat German-built Rohrbach Roland trimotor.

Under commercial pressure the airlines merged in 1929 to form an operation called Compañía de Líneas Aéreas Subvencionadas SA or "CLASSA", with technical and financial backing provided by Deutsche Lufthansa. Two years later the name changed again, this time to LAPE or Líneas Aéreas Postales Españolas. In 1933 LAPE began a scheduled passenger service to Las Palmas in the Canaries. In 1936, just as the

civil war in Spain was beginning, the airline ordered Douglas DC-2s. For four years the bitter fighting severely truncated the development of air transport. In 1940 the victorious nationalist government reorganized the airline as Iberia – Líneas Aéreas de España – with a handful of DH 84 Dragons and a fleet of Junkers Ju 52/3m. In 1943 three DC-3s were delivered from the US. That same year the airline was fully nationalized through the state-owned Instituto Nacional de Industria.

Postwar, the airline's equipment was largely made up of DC-3s and some DC-4s which opened the first routes to Latin America in 1949. Lockheed L-1049G Super Constellations began a Madrid-New York service in 1954. The first jets, Caravelles and Douglas DC-8-50s, were acquired in 1961.

Above left
An Airbus A300 waiting to take off at London, Heathrow

Above
A Boeing 727-200 retracts its undercarriage shortly after take-off from Palma

Iberia

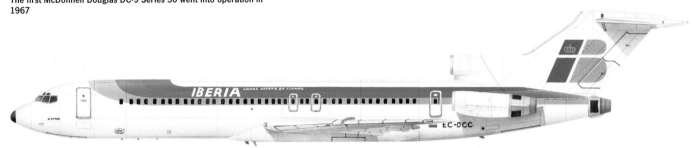

continued

Iberia became a major shareholder in the charter operator Viva Air, jointly owned with Lufthansa, but in 1990 the German airline's shareholding was bought out. Viva Air now operates scheduled services from Palma, Majorca. Also in 1990 Iberia established a subsidiary airline called Binter Canarias to operate scheduled passenger services to the Canary Islands, previously provided by Aviaco. In late 1990 the airline bought a substantial shareholding in Aerolíneas Argentinas.

Iberia flies an extensive domestic network within Spain and international scheduled passenger and cargo services to the Americas, Africa, Europe, and the Middle and Far East.

Fleet: eight Airbus A300B4, six A320, four Boeing 747-200B, three Boeing 747-200 Combi, 35 Boeing 727-200, eight McDonnell Douglas DC-10-30, 19 McDonnell Douglas DC-9-30, 17 McDonnell Douglas MD-87, 2 MD-83; On order, eight Airbus 340, eight A321, 15 Airbus A320, 7 McDonnell Douglas MD-87, 16 Boeing 757-200

Above
A McDonnell Douglas DC-10

Japan Air Lines (JAL)

The major airline of Japan was formed in 1951 as the future Pacific economic superpower began to emerge from its period of immediate postwar reconstruction. It initially relied on help from Northwest Airlines, but in 1953 half the shareholding was acquired by the state and the airline began to expand both its domestic operations and to push out routes to overseas destinations. In 1954 the first international service was opened – from Tokyo to San Francisco via Wake Island and Honolulu, using DC-6Bs and, later, DC-7Cs.

As domestic competition intensified in the early 1960s, the government nudged JAL towards a global marketplace, opening up a route to Europe via the North Pole and another via India in 1961-2. The first pure jets were Convair CV880s, and later DC-8-50s and -62 Series. The first wide-body Boeing 747s entered service with the Japanese flag-carrier in 1976.

In April 1990 JAL took convertible options on the McDonnell Douglas MD-12, a proposed stretched version of the MD-11, capable of carrying 441 second-class passengers. The airline has two subsidiaries, Japan

continued

Asia Airways formed in 1975 to fly from Japanese cities to Taipei, capital of Taiwan, and South West Airlines servicing destinations on Okinawa and in the Ryukyu island chain.

JAL operates scheduled passenger and freight services to Brisbane, Cairns, Perth, Sydney, Auckland, Anchorage, Vancouver, Seattle, Atlanta, San Francisco, Los Angeles, Chicago, New York, Mexico City, Rio de Janeiro, São Paulo, London, Paris, Amsterdam, Düsseldorf, Copenhagen, Hamburg, Frankfurt, Zurich, Rome, Athens and Madrid.

Fleet: ten Boeing 747-400, eight Boeing 747-300, 23 747-200, nine

Page 71, above
A Boeing 747-400 in JAL's new corporate livery
Page 71, below
A McDonnell Douglas DC-10-40
Above
A Boeing 747-400
Right
The old livery on a Boeing 747

747-200F, 13 747SR, five 747-100, one 747-100F, 17 McDonnell Douglas DC-10-40, three Boeing 767-200, ten Boeing 767-300; On order 29 747-400, 10 McDonnell Douglas MD-11

KLM KONINKLIJKE LUCHVAART MAATSCHAPPIJ NV

The national flag-carrier of the Netherlands is the oldest operating airline in the world. Founded in 1919, it began operations in 1920 with a service from Amsterdam to London using four-passenger DH16s. During the 1920s the operation spread across Europe and in 1929 an air route was opened to the Dutch East Indies. The eight-point route, flown by Fokker FVIIIs from Amsterdam to Batavia on the island of Java (later Djakarta), was at the time the longest regular air service in the world.

The advanced DC-2 airliner went into service with KLM (the first European airline to operate this aircraft) in 1934, the year the airline forged its first transatlantic link with a route to Curaçao using a Fokker FXVIII. In 1936 KLM was the first European airline to order the DC-3. In 1935 intra-Caribbean services were started from the Netherlands Antilles.

These continued unbroken during World War II allowing KLM to claim over 65 years of continuous operations. Some aircraft escaped the German invasion, to fly a wartime route from Bristol to Gibraltar via Lisbon under charter to BOAC. The new Lockheed Lodestars ordered by the company were diverted to the Caribbean where they opened a service to Miami in 1943.

With a fleet of refurbished DC-3s and DC-4s the airline struggled to start up again after the ravages of war. The link to Batavia was renewed in November 1945, New York joined the route network in 1946, and Rio and Buenos Aires were on KLM's map by 1948 as long-range Constellations and DC-6s joined the fleet. Turboprop Vickers Viscounts began to operate the European routes in 1957, to be joined by Lockheed Electras ten years later. The first pure-jets, Douglas DC-8-30s,

went into service in 1960. DC-9s progressively began to replace the Viscounts and Electras from 1966 onwards. These in turn have been replaced with Boeing 737s. In 1966 KLM established a domestic subsidiary called NLM which linked Amsterdam with Gronigen, Enschede, Eindhoven and Maastricht with a fleet of twin prop Fokker F27 Friendships.

KLM has a 14.9% shareholding in Air UK which provides feeder services into Amsterdam from nine UK regional airports. It also operates Netherlines as part of NLM, its fully owned domestic subsidiary and all aircraft are flown in the NLM Cityhopper livery. The airline also has a 40% stake in the charter operator, Transavia. Plans to join Sabena and BA in a new European venture called Sabena World Airways were aborted at the end of 1990.

KLM today operates a network of scheduled passenger and cargo

Above left
A Boeing 747-400

Above
Airbus A310

services from its Schipol headquarters to 142 cities in 77 countries worldwide.

Fleet: ten Airbus A310-200, eight Boeing 747-400, 13 Boeing 747-300, four 747-200B, six 737-400, 13 737-300, five McDonnell-Douglas DC-10-30; On order; seven Boeing 747-400, two 747F, seven 737-400, ten MD-11.
KLM CityHopper: eight Fokker 50, four F28-4000, three F27-500, ten Saab 340; On order, two Fokker 50, three Saab 340.

Korean Air

The flag carrier of South Korea was formed in 1962 and today is one of the fastest-growing airlines in the world with significant numbers of aircraft on order. It is the successor to Korean National Airlines, which had been founded in 1947 by the Ministry of Transport. The Korean War temporarily ended operations, which began again in 1952. The airline started to fly a domestic network within South Korea and to Hong Kong, with a small fleet of DC-3s, DC-4s and a single Lockheed Constellation. Later two Super Constellations were acquired in the 1960s and remained in service until the first jets (DC-9s) were delivered in 1967.

The airline was sold to private commercial interests in 1969 and began a period of rapid and still accelerating expansion, acquiring a large fleet of Boeing 707s, 727s and 747s and later Airbus A300s and MD-82s. In 1983 a KAL Boeing 747 was tragically shot down when it strayed over Soviet air defenses northwest of Japan.

Domestic scheduled passenger services are operated from Seoul to Cheju and Pusan with international services to Frankfurt, London, Paris, Vienna, Zurich, Los Angeles, New York, Toronto, Vancouver, Bahrain, Jeddah, Riyadh, Bangkok, Fukuoka, Hong Kong, Kuala Lumpur, Manila, Nagasaki, Nagoya, Nigata, Osaka, Sapporo, Singapore, Taipei and Tokyo.

Fleet: five Boeing 747-400, three 747-300, one 747-300 Combi, seven 747-200B, one 747-200 Combi, six 747-200F, two 747SP, ten Boeing 727-200, three McDonnell-Douglas DC-10-30, ten Airbus A300B4, twelve A300-600, four Fokker F.28-4000, one F.27-500, one McDonnell Douglas MD-11, eight McDonnell-Douglas MD-82; On order, twenty-five Boeing 747-400, four MD-11, two MD-82, nine Airbus A300-600R.

Above left
A McDonnell Douglas MD-11

Above
A Boeing 747-200F, windowless cargo version, at Los Angeles

Lufthansa DEUTSCHE LUFTHANSA AG

On 28 October 1990 a Lufthansa Airbus A310 landed at Berlin's Tempelhof airport, formally re-establishing services to the former capital by a reunited Germany's national airline. The occasion was another dramatic milestone for the airline which has often been at the center of turbulent historic events.

Indeed, the world's first commercial air transport venture was formed in Germany. In 1909, the Deutsche Luftschiffahrts AG, or DELAG, was formed to operate Zeppelin airships. The coming of war ended the dream of giant dirigibles gracefully crossing the skies of Europe. They did just that in four years of fighting, but carrying bombs not passengers.

Germany's civil air transport and technically advanced aircraft industry managed to pick themselves up quickly from the ruins of defeat in 1918. The Commission Aéronautique Inter-Alliée meanwhile strove to make sure that the provisions of the Versailles Treaty banning military aviation were being adhered to.

The winged crest of today's giant airline is that adopted by the Luftrederei company formed in 1919. By 1925 two major airline groupings had emerged – Deutsche Aero-Lloyd AG and the Junkers Luftverkehr AG, the latter effectively controlled by the state government. In January 1926 the two operations merged as Deutsche Luft-Hansa AG and services began in April with a fleet of Junkers, Dorniers and Fokkers

reaching out across Germany and to East Prussia and neighboring countries. In July-September 1926 three Junkers G24 trimotors left Berlin and flew to Peking and back with the object of exploring the possibility of establishing a regular Deutsche Lufthansa service across Asia. An agreement with the Chinese government allowed the airline to develop an air service within China, with a hub at Nanking. In 1931 the Eurasia Aviation Corporation opened an air mail route from Shanghai to Peking. In 1933 a route from Berlin to Shanghai via Soviet Siberia was opened.

Deutsche Lufthansa had a substantial holding in the Kondor Syndikat formed in 1924 to nurture airlines and German commercial interests in several Latin American countries. Kondor was particularly active in Brazil and pioneered a route across the South Atlantic, linking Berlin with South America. The operation was nationalized by Brazil (now at war with Germany) in 1942.

Meanwhile, during the early 1930s the airline was spreading its routes out across Europe and bringing new aircraft into the fleet such as the Junkers G31 (on which the world's first in-flight meal service was introduced), the Ju 52/3m and the 34-passenger Junkers G38. The coming to power of the Nazis in 1933 led to the airline being suborned to the political and military interests of the state. There was increased pressure to expand while new, advanced aircraft such as the Ju 86

continued

were developed in parallel as bombers. In 1938 a Focke-Wulf Fw 200 (also later adapted as a maritime reconnaissance bomber) made a non-stop Berlin-New York flight but this never became a regular scheduled passenger service.

The coming of war stunted Lufthansa's growth. Defeat stripped it of its interests in Asia and Latin America and left it completely shattered in Europe. Under the Allied Control Commission's direction it was left to BEA, Pan American and Air France to re-establish domestic links within what became West Germany and connections with West Berlin – services they continued to operate until 1990. Then in January 1953 the West German government established a new operation called Aktiengesellschaft für Luftverkehrsbedarf or Luftag, with a maintenance base at Hamburg. The airline grew quickly, becoming part of the country's economic miracle. Convair CV340s began to operate European routes and Super Constellations opened a regular Frankfurt-New York service in 1955. In East Berlin an airline called Deutsche Lufthansa (later Interflug) was set up in 1954.

However, in West Germany the company had also by now revived the name Lufthansa. The first jets, Boeing 707-430s, arrived in 1960 – and the routes network began to stretch out to Africa and Australia. Boeing 727s started to supplant Viscounts on the European and domestic routes in 1964. It was the first non-US airline to order the Boeing 737, in 1965. Lufthansa was also the first European operator of the Boeing 747, taking delivery of its first wide-body in March 1970. DC-10s followed in 1972 and Airbus A300B4s in 1977, a European aircraft with a very important German-built component, once again joining the fleet. Flights to East Germany, linking Frankfurt and Leipzig were begun on 10 August 1989.

Today Lufthansa, 65% owned by the Federal German government, is one of Europe's largest carriers. It has a plan to double the capacity of the airline of a newly reunited Germany within 12 years. It is a launch customer for the Airbus A340 which will replace its DC-10s. The airline

Page 78
An Airbus A310-200
Page 79
A Boeing 747 in its all-freight version
Above
Tail of a Boeing 727-200

has recently formed an air freight subsidiary, called German Cargo. The fleet includes two Boeing 747s and two 737s. Condor Flugdienst is another subsidiary which operates charter and international flights.

The airline flies a global network of scheduled passenger and cargo services to 178 destinations in 84 countries in Europe, Africa, Asia, Australasia and North, Central and South America.

Fleet: ten Boeing 747-400, 12 Boeing 747-200B Combi, five Boeing 747-200B, five 747-200F, 11 McDonnell-Douglas DC-10-30, ten Airbus A300-600, twelve Airbus A310-200, eight Airbus A310-300, seventeen Airbus A320, 19 Boeing 727-200, 3 Boeing 737-500, 23 Boeing 737-300, 40 737-200, two 737-200C; On order, two Airbus A300-600, two Airbus A310-300, 13 Airbus A320, 20 A321, 15 A340, four Boeing 747-400, six 737-300, 33 737-500

Malaysia Airlines

Above
A Boeing 737-200

The forerunner to Malaysia Airlines, Malayan Airways was originally founded in 1947 using Airspeed Consuls flying from Singapore via Kuala Lumpur to Penang. In the immediate post-colonial period of the late 1950s Malayan Airways Ltd (formed in 1958), with its headquarters in Singapore, was jointly owned by BOAC, Qantas and by the newly independent governments of Singapore, Malaya, Sarawak, Brunei and North Borneo. The airline flew DC-3s locally and (from 1960) Constellations and Britannias on international routes. Jet services began with Comets leased from BOAC in 1962.

During 1963-67 the carrier operated as Malaysian Airlines, and from 1967 to 1971 as Malaysia-Singapore airlines. During this period the Comets were replaced with Boeing 737s and 707s. In 1971 Malaysia Airlines was formed out of the old consortium when Singapore opted out in order to form its own national airline (cf Singapore Airlines).

Operations began the following year under the banner Malaysian Airlines System (MAS) and the name changed to its present form in 1987. At the end of 1990 the airline announced plans to develop the northern Malaysian city of Johore Bahru as a domestic and international air travel base, following government plans to upgrade the airport at nearby Senai.

In the same year several South East Asian carriers, including Malay-sia, Thai, Garuda, Singapore and Royal Brunei, set up a working group to examine commercial co-operation between them. In January 1991 Malaysia ordered 10 Boeing 737-400s and took options on ten more. The carrier also firmed up two of its eight options for Airbus A330s and ordered another Fokker 50.

The airline operates from its Kuala Lumpur base to 38 domestic destinations and to Singapore, Djakarta, Beijing, Medan, Manila, Phuket, Hong Kong, Taipei, Tokyo, Dubai, Amman, Colombo, Bangkok, Melbourne, Perth, Sydney, Delhi, Zurich, Madras, Seoul, Honolulu, Los Angeles, Amsterdam, Jeddah, London, Frankfurt, Paris and Mauritius. The airline is the parent of Pelangi Air, a new domestic airline with a fleet of Dornier 228s.

Fleet: five Airbus A300B4, one Boeing 747-400, two 747-400 Combi, one 747-300 Combi, 13 737-200, five Boeing Canada DHC-6 Twin Otter, ten Fokker 50, six McDonnell Douglas Dc-10-30; On order: 10 Airbus A330-300, 20 Boeing 737-400, six 737-500, six Boeing 747-400.

Northwest is a major US carrier, with its traffic hubs at Detroit, Minneapolis/St Paul and Memphis.

It was founded in 1926 as an air mail carrier and operated between Detroit and Minneapolis/St Paul using three Stinsons. Locked out of the 1930 agreement to give US Mail contracts to a handful of operators, Northwest struggled to keep airborne until the mail routes were reallocated in 1934. Slowly the airline, now called Northwest Orient, began to build a spreading route network using a wide collection of aircraft, including Hamilton monoplanes, Ford trimotors, Lockeed Orions, Beech Travelairs, Lockheed Electras and Lockheed L14s. DC-3s were introduced in 1939. In 1942 the bulk of Northwest's fleet was committed to support of military operations in Alaska and the northern Pacific. In the postwar period the acquisition of a fleet of DC-4s and DC-6Bs allowed Northwest to build a transcontinental route

network within the US, flying from New York and Washington to Portland and Seattle and out across the Pacific to Alaska, Hawaii, Japan and Korea. Boeing Stratocruisers were acquired in 1949 for the long-haul routes, DC-7Cs and Super Constellations following in the mid-1950s.

The company ordered Martin 2-0-2s as replacements for the DC-3s on its domestic routes but a series of accidents caused the fleet to be grounded. The first turboprops were Lockheed Electras (introduced in 1959) and the first pure-jets, Douglas DC-8-30s, went into operation in 1960 followed two years later by Boeing 720Bs. Wide-body 747-100s joined the Northwest Orient fleet in 1972 followed by DC-10-10s. After deregulation of the US airline industry in the late 1970s Northwest moved vigorously to build up its route network, opening a service from Chicago to Tokyo and all-cargo flights across the North Atlantic. North-

west almost doubled in size when it took over Republic Airlines with a fleet of 170 aircraft in 1986.

The airline was the launch customer for the Boeing 747-400 in 1989 when the first of these new-generation, fuel-efficient 400+-seaters went into service on the transpacific routes. Northwest also has large numbers of Airbus aircraft on order. In 1985 the operation was commercially restructured and retitled simply Northwest Airlines. It has marketing agreements with several commuter airlines – Express, Horizon Air, Mesaba, Northeast Express and Precision – which feed passengers to the hubs under the banner "Northwest Airlink."

Northwest flies a large domestic network within the US and in Canada. The airline flies internationally to Hawaii, Tokyo, Osaka, Seoul, Okinawa, Taipei, Manila, Hong Kong, Shanghai, Guam, Singapore, Saipan and Bangkok, London, Glasgow, Frankfurt, Paris, Amsterdam, Cancun,

Above left
A McDonnell Douglas DC-9 Series 30 showing the new 1989 livery, at Miami

Above
A Boeing 747-400, the latest version of the giant carrier, at Phoenix, Arizona

Montego Bay and the Cayman Islands.

Fleet: 15 Airbus A320-200, 12 Boeing 747-100, 20 747-200, eight 747-200F, ten 747-400, 21 DC-10-40, 33 Boeing 757-200, 70 Boeing 727-100/200, eight McDonnell-Douglas MD-82, 33 McDonnell-Douglas DC-9-10, 77 DC-9-30, four DC-9-40, 28 DC-9-50; On order; 85 Airbus A320-200, 16 A330, 20 A340, six Boeing 747-400, 40 757-200.

Olympic OLYMPIC AIRWAYS

The national airline of Greece has a troubled commercial history. Now wholly government-owned, Olympic was founded in 1957 by the shipping tycoon, Aristotle Onassis, who took over the routes operated by Greek National Airlines (TAE) and Hellenic Airlines. TAE itself had been created in 1951 through a merger with Hellas and Aero Metafoa Ellados and TAE itself. The resulting airline was nationalized three years later.

Onassis was granted a 50-year concession with a monopoly on domestic routes and authority to operate the national flag carrier internationally. Operations began to points in Europe and the Near East with a fleet of DC-3, DC-4s and, from 1957, the first DC-6Bs flying a route from Athens to London via Rome and Paris. Comet 4Bs went into service in 1960. Boeing 707s inaugurated a non-stop Athens-New York service in July 1966.

The 1960s were prosperous for Olympic. Boeing 727s were brought in on European routes, Japanese-built NAMC YS-11As replaced the DC-3s on local networks and five 720Bs supplanted the DC-6Bs on the long-haul flights. But the level of commercial cosseting afforded by the state could not guarantee profitability. With a fanfare Boeing 747-200Bs inaugurated both Athens-New York and Athens-Sydney services

in June 1973 but by now, hit by the steep rise in fuel costs, the airline was losing a lot of money.

After heavy losses Onassis withdrew in 1974. The airline virtually ceased to operate until it was reorganized, and resumed flying under state ownership in 1976. In 1979 the airline embarked on a new aircraft acquisition program, basing its inter-Europe operations on Airbuses, its domestic short haul on the Boeing 737 and its intercontinental services on the 747.

Today Olympic operates scheduled passenger services to 31 cities and island destinations in Greece and to 39 destinations in Europe, Africa, Asia and North America. The first of six new Boeing 737-400s was delivered in September 1991.

Fleet: eight Airbus A300 B4; four Boeing 747-200B, one Boeing 737-400, nine Boeing 727-200, 11 Boeing 737-200. On order; two Airbus A300-600R, five Boeing 737-400.

Pan Am   PAN AMERICAN WORLD AIRWAYS

A dominant force in world aviation for over 60 years, at the outset of the 1990s Pan Am flew into the financial turbulence facing many airlines, hampered by a crippling legacy of losses made during the preceding decade. In order to stay solvent it has sold off many of its assets, including routes and aircraft, a typical example being the sale of its routes from Heathrow to United in a $40 million deal, and its continued existence is very much in doubt.*

Pan American World Airways was founded on 28 October 1927 with the ambitious aim of opening up international services to South America and the Caribbean. The first service was flown from Key West to Cuba using a Fairchild FC-2 seaplane carrying mail. Very soon its was replaced by a Fokker FVII trimotor landplane. The first passengers were carried in January 1928 but already the airline's founder, the dynamic Juan Trippe, was peering further south anxious to compete with growing German influence in the potentially vast market of Central and South America. A contract from the US Mail gave Pan Am a monopoly of international air mail operations and within 18 months PAA was operating a route network of 12,000 miles. The flying boats dubbed

Pan Am

continued

"Clippers" by a management which wrote much of the airline marketing book in that heady period, dominated the PAA fleet as it grew during the 1930s. Sikorsky S42s and S43s, Martin M130s and, later, giant Boeing 314s, began to span the Atlantic and Pacific oceans.

In South America the expansion of PAA proceeded by way of buy-up deals and a series of mergers. Pan American Grace Airways, or Panagra, was formed in conjunction with the Grace shipping line to operate in Peru, Chile and Bolivia. PAA-owned Avianca had a near monopoly in Colombia. When the Brazilian government demanded local ownership of airlines, PAA bought a stake in Panair do Brasil.

America's war in Europe and the Pacific made great calls on PAA's transport fleet. Postwar PAA ended its great flying boat tradition, switching first to the DC-4 and then rushing to get into service the new aircraft on offer by US manufacturers. PAA was first in the air with the great propliners of the period – the Constellation, the DC-6 and the Boeing Stratocruiser. In 1956 the Douglas DC-7C was introduced, which could fly the Atlantic from New York to western European capitals with only one intermediate refueling stop.

Pan Am ordered the Boeing 707 in 1955 just a year after the first flight of the revolutionary Boeing Jet Transport and flew the first revenue-earning flight, from New York to Paris on 26 October 1958. PAA was to operate 707s until October 1983. The Pan Am order started the rush for the aircraft which, although preceded into scheduled passenger service by the DH Comet, was the true begetter of the jet age in civil air transport. Pan Am was first, too, into the wide-body age, placing an order for 25 Boeing 747s, off the drawing board in 1966. The first 747-121 started commercial service with a non-stop flights from New York to London on 21 January 1970.

PAA was denied a domestic network – it could not even operate transcontinental-US connecting flights, but deregulation at the end of the 1970s allowed it to build a domestic service. A short cut to this objective was provided when Pan Am took control of Miami-based

Page 86
An Airbus A310-300
Page 87, above
A Boeing 737-200
Page 87, below
A Boeing 727
Above Douglas DC-6

National Airlines with a large route network around the eastern seaboard and Gulf coast, plus ready-made trans-US services. In 1986 the airline sold its entire Pacific division to United Airlines.

The airline acquired Ransome Airlines in 1986, turning it into a feeder operation called Pan Am Express to service its New York hubs and West Berlin's Tegel airport where the carrier retained rights to operate domestic services to West Germany.

Pan Am operates scheduled passenger services to the Caribbean, South America, Europe, the Middle East, Africa and the Far East.

*On 4 December 1991, following the breakdown of rescue package negotiations with Delta Airlines, Pan Am grounded its aircraft and ceased trading. At the time of going to press it seemed unlikely that the 64-year-old airline would be rescued.

Fleet: seven Boeing 747-200B, 27 Boeing 747-100, 13 Airbus A300B4, seven A310-200, 14 Airbus A310-300, 89 Boeing 727-100/200, five Boeing 737-200.

Philippine Airlines

Above
A Boeing 747 at London, Gatwick, showing the current airline trend towards simplified but striking colors (1989)

The national carrier of the Philippines was formed in 1941 by the entrepreneur Andre Sorianao, just before the outbreak of the Pacific War, to operate domestic services only. Operations were resumed in 1946 with one route between Manila and Legaspi, but soon spread out among the myriad islands that make up the sprawling country with its teeming population. International flights started a year later, with a route from Manila to California via Guam, Wake Island and Honolulu using DC-4s and DC-6s, but these were suspended in 1954. A service was maintained with Hong Kong with DC-6s and later with Viscounts.

Domestic network equipment included DC-3s, DHC Otters and Scottish Aviation Twin Pioneers hopping between 72 points on the islands, many of them just strips in the jungle. Viscounts and Fokker F27s arrived in the late 1950s and DC-8s in 1962 to begin international operations once more. The airline was nationalized in 1977.

The airline today flies a 42-point domestic network and international scheduled passenger services to Singapore, Kuala Lumpur, Taipei, Hong Kong, Honolulu, San Francisco, Los Angeles, Tokyo, Melbourne, Sydney, Brisbane, Ho Chi Minh City, Jakarta, Bangkok, Karachi, Rome, Frankfurt, Amsterdam, Paris, Beijing, Xiamen, Dharan, Dubai, Bahrain, Riyadh and London.

Fleet: nine Boeing 747-200B, nine Boeing 737-300, two McDonnell-Douglas DC-10-30, seven Airbus A300B4, four One-Eleven 500, seven Shorts 360-300, ten Fokker 50; On order: four Boeing 737-300.

Australia's national long-haul airline can trace its roots back to 1920 when the company was founded as Queensland and Northern Territory Aerial Services. With just an Avro 504K and a Royal Aircraft Factory BE2e the fledgling airline began flying mail services between dusty wool towns. In 1928 Q.A.N.T.A.S. began the first scheduled air service in Australia – the 80 miles from Brisbane to Toowoomba. The same year the Flying Doctor service was inaugurated.

In 1934 the airline started operating the Singapore-Brisbane sector of the new Imperial Airways mail route between Britain and Australia. De Havilland DH86s in the livery of Qantas Empire Airways began the service and, after some initial technical snags, the service settled down – flying a long overwater hop from Timor to Singapore. The journey from Brisbane to London's Croydon airport took between 12 and 14 days. In 1938 Qantas was re-equipped with 'C' class Empire flying boats and moved its headquarters to Sydney. The journey time for the Southampton-Sydney flying boat service was cut to nine and a half days. Eventually there were six 'C' class in service.

The airline made a major contribution to the Australian war effort in the Pacific. Qantas flying boats ferried men and equipment into New Guinea where Australian troops held the southern flank of the Japanese advance. The airline also managed to operate Catalinas across the Pacific and to Ceylon (Sri Lanka) on a journey that took 28 hours in the air. The building of an airstrip on the Cocos Islands permitted landplanes take over the London-Sydney journey, allowing a break between Perth and Ceylon. At the end of the war Qantas flew a motley collection of aircraft, including DC-3s, Liberators, Lancastrians and DH Dragons, as well as various flying boats.

In October 1947 Lockheed Constellations took over on the so-called 'Kangaroo Route' flying London-Sydney in four days, with stops at Cairo

Left and right
Nose and tail views of a Boeing 747-300

and Singapore. That year the government of the Commonwealth of Australia bought out first BOAC's 50% shareholding, then the rest of the airline.

In the 1950s the airline introduced Super Constellations and opened new routes to the Philippines and Japan. A service was opened to Johannesburg via Mauritius in 1952. Five years later the airline was granted route authority to fly a round-the-world service from Sydney to San Francisco, New York and London. The first jets, long-range short-fuselage Boeing 707-138s, went into service in 1959 and had supplanted the Super Constellations by 1964. The company bought Lockheed Electra turboprops in 1960 to fly its regional and Asian routes and services across the Tasman Sea to New Zealand. The airline's first 747-200Bs entered service in 1973, and they still provide the backbone of the all-Boeing fleet. Two short-fuselage 747SPs were acquired to fly the less frequented routes to the smaller Australian and New Zealand cities.

In November 1990 Qantas decided to sell its older 747s in a bid to raise cash in the build-up to the airline's proposed privatization and the deregulation of the Australian airline industry. Subsequently seven were sold in early 1991 to leasing companies for use by United Airlines.

The airline operates scheduled passenger services from Sydney, Melbourne, Brisbane, Adelaide, Perth, Hobart, Cairns, Townsville, Port Headland and Norfolk Island to London, Manchester, Amsterdam, Frankfurt, Rome, Harare, Singapore, Bangkok, Phuket, Kuala Lumpur, Jakarta, Denpasar, Hong Kong, Tokyo, Nagoya, Fukuoka, Wellington, Christchurch, Nadi, Nouméa, Paeete, Honolulu, Los Angeles, San Francisco, New York, Vancouver and Buenos Aires.

Fleet: nine Boeing 747-400, six 747-300, 11 747-200B, two 747-200 Combi, two 747SP, one 747-100, eight 767-300ER, seven 767-200ER. On order, four Boeing 747-400, four 767-300ER

Sabena SOCIÉTÉ ANONYME BELGE D'EXPLOITATION DE LA NAVIGATION AÉRIENNE

The flag carrier of Belgium, the Société Annonyme Belge d'Exploitation de la Navigation Aerienne or SABENA was founded in Brussels in 1923. It replaced a short-lived operation called the Syndicat National pour l'Etude de Transport Aérien or SNETA. This pioneering airline had begun operations in 1920 with a collection of converted war-surplus aircraft, including a Fokker FVII, de Havilland DH9As and Rumpler CIVs, flying services from Brussels to Paris and Brussels to London.

In the country's huge African colony, the Belgian Congo, SNETA operated the ''King Albert Airline'' with three-seat Georges Lévy G.L. 40 flying boats servicing a route from the coast at Léopoldville along the line of the Congo river to Stanleyville in the interior.

SNETA was really a route-proving operation. Sabena was an airline proper which started a scheduled freight operation from Rotterdam to Strasbourg via Brussels on 1 April 1924. A trimotor Handley-Page W9e was delivered soon afterwards to open up scheduled passenger services to Amsterdam, Basle and Antwerp. Two more followed in 1925, built in Belgium, plus eight more of the big, awkward-looking biplanes to operate a direct overland service from Léopoldville in the Congo. In February 1925 a W8e made a multiple-stop, route-proving flight from Brussels to Léopoldville, but it was to be another ten years before a regular Belgium-Congo service was opened – using Fokker FVIIs. By the outbreak of war the mainstay of Sabena's European-dedicated fleet was the Ju52/3m and another trimotor, the Savoia-Marchetti SM73.

Belgium was occupied by the Germans in 1940 and, as the invaders approached, several crews managed to seek refuge with their aircraft in Britain. In the Congo, operations initially ceased, then restarted with new links to Khartoum and Cairo. The link to Europe, now terminating in Marseilles in Vichy France, was broken in when the Germans occupied the whole of France in 1943. In 1944 it was reopened – this time from the Congo via Casablanca and Lisbon to London. In July 1945 a Lockheed Lodestar reopened the link from Léopoldville to liberated Brussels.

In common with other postwar airlines, the Douglas DC-3 was the backbone of a rebuilt Sabena fleet, now reaching out again all over

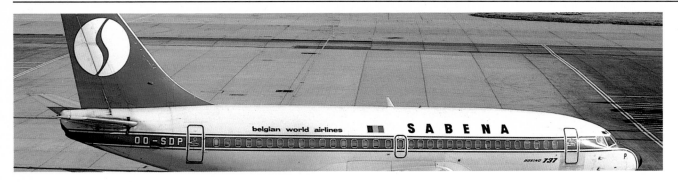

Europe. DC-4s opened a Brussels-New York service in 1947 and in 1953 the airline initiated a pioneering passenger helicopter service, using Sikorsky S55s. At the same period Convair CV240s began to supplant the DC-3s on the European routes, and DC-6As and Bs took up the long-haul routes. In 1957 Douglas DC-7Cs joined the fleet and went into service on the North Atlantic.

The jet age arrived for Sabena in 1960 with the entry into service of four Boeing 707-329s. The following year six Caravelle VIs began operation on Sabena's European routes. In 1960 the Belgian Congo had become independent and the company's route network was handed over the to the new Air Congo (later Air Zaïre). The breakaway province of Katanga briefly operated some Sabena DC-3s.

Today Sabena's modern Airbus- and Boeing-based fleet flies all over Europe, to points in the Middle and Far East, and to 26 destinations in Africa. Scheduled passenger services are flown to Montreal, New York, Atlanta, Detroit, Chicago, Boston, Toronto and Anchorage.

Sabena has important subsidiaries including the charter and inclusive-tour operation Sobelair (founded in 1946 to operate charter flights, largely to the Congo), Société Transair and several hotel, catering and service companies. In 1990 the company embarked on a ambi-

Page 92
McDonnell Douglas DC-10

Page 93
A Boeing 747-200 at Atlanta, Georgia
Above
A Boeing 737-200 (1985)

tious plan to set up a new operation called Sabena World Airways, with British Airways and KLM each holding a 20% stake. The plan was to create by 1995 an extensive intra-European network servicing 75 cities and feeding a new hub at Brussels-Zaventum airport. Rising fuel costs, the Gulf crisis and the airline industry recession caused the postponement of the project at the beginning of 1991, and British Airways is now facing competition from Air France in its plan to invest in Sabena in order to gain access to its vital Brussels European hub.

Fleet: one Airbus A310-300, two A310-200; two Boeing 747-300 Combi, one 747-100 Combi, one Boeing 737-500, six Boeing 737-300, 13 737-200, five McDonnell Douglas DC-10-30CF; on order ten A340-300, one 737-300, three 737-400, 121737-500.

The flag-carrier of Saudi Arabia was founded in 1945 with a single DC-3, the personal gift of the US president, Roosevelt, to the king. The airline began operations in 1947 with a service between Riyadh and the summer capital, Jeddah. In the 1950s, although it was owned by the Saudi Arabian government, management and technical services for the growing airline were provided by TWA. The fleet expanded to include Convair 340s, DC-4s and Bristol 170 freighters. Since the early 1960s the airline's fleet and route network has grown exponentially in size, in step with the nation's oil wealth. Today it is the largest carrier in the Middle East.

Saudia operates scheduled passenger and freight services to 23 domestic destinations within the county from its main hub at Jeddah. International services are flown from Jeddah, from the capital Riyadh, and from Dharan to 51 destinations in Europe, Africa, the Middle and Far East and North America. The Gulf war of 1991 severely disrupted the airline's operations.

Fleet: 11 Boeing 747-300, one 747-200F, three 747SP, eight 747-100, 11 Airbus A300-600, 20 Boeing 737-200, two Boeing 737-200C, 17 Lockheed L-1011 TriStar 200, one Tristar 500, one DC-8-63F, one DC-8, five Gulfstream II, six Gulfstream III, two Gulfstream IV, one Falcon 900, two Cessna Citation, two Beech King Air A-100.

The joint airline of Scandinavia was founded in 1946 when Norwegian, Danish and Swedish interests came together to operate international services. Later SAS assumed responsibility for all the activities of its founder airlines, DDL, DNL and ABA. It is a rare example of a collaborative, multi-national effort to run an airline which has survived time, commercial vicissitudes and no lack of internal disagreements.

The three founder airlines were Det Danske Luftfartselskap (DDL) of Denmark, Det Norske Luftfartselskap of Norway (DNL) and AB Aerotransport (ABA) of Sweden, all of which were formed in the early 1920s, except for DDL, formed in 1918. Ownership is still vested in these holding companies in the proportion 2:2:3. In turn, each company is 50% state-owned, the remainder of the shares being held by individuals or investment institutions.

Discussion between the three managements began in the 1930s at the time of the opening of a northern great circle route across the Atlantic to North America in competition with the routes opening up via the Azores and Ireland. Early in 1940 an agreement was reached with Pan American to do just this – but subject to the formation of a single Scandinavian body with which PAA could deal. The German invasion of Denmark and Norway put an end to the project. During the occupation DDL operated fitfully under Nazi control. The Norwegian carrier was completely grounded, while civil air transport continued in neutral Sweden. In 1946, after long negotiations, the prewar plan for a cooperative agreement was revived.

On 17 September 1946 a DC-4 wearing the new legend – Scandina-

vian Airlines System – left Stockholm for New York. Soon a route to Montevideo was opened, followed by Buenos Aires. In the early 1950s the route network spread to destinations in Asia. In 1951 the airline pioneered the Polar route from Stockholm to Tokyo. New aircraft joined the fleet in this last golden age of piston-powered air travel – DC6Bs and DC7Cs for the transatlantic routes, while Short Sandringham flying boats proved useful operating along Norway's coastal fjords. Fleet registrations were divided among the three member countries.

The first jets, Douglas DC-8-30s, went into service in 1960. SAS has achieved its very significant growth through a series of strategic marketing and traffic alliances all over the world. In 1962 SAS played a major role in the establishment of Thai Airways and retains a hub at Bangkok. There is a marketing alliance with Varig of Brazil providing access to a South American network. Since 1988 SAS has had a 10% holding in the US major, Continental Airlines, which has provided a vital access to the huge US market. In 1989 SAS bought 24.9% of Airlines of Britain Holdings, parent company of British Midland, and the joint-airline agreed with All Nippon Airlines for joint venture service between Japan and Scandinavia. In late 1990 SAS opened a strategic business department with a brief to look for further new partnerships.

SAS has subsidiary interests in hotels, catering and service companies. It wholly owns the charter airline Scanair, which flies from Stockholm, Malmö, Göteborg, Oslo and Copenhagen to leisure resorts with a fleet of six McDonnell Douglas DC-10-10s. There are holdings in the airlines Danair, Linjeflyg (share sold in 1990/91), Greenlandair, Helikopter Service, Widere and Spanair.

SAS flies an extensive intra-Scandinavian route network of scheduled passenger services to the major cities of Europe, Africa, the Near, Middle and Far East, and the Americas.

Fleet: Ten Boeing 767-300ER, two Boeing 767-200ER, eighteen McDonnell Douglas MD-81, eleven MD-82, eleven MD-83, eight MD-87, one McDonnell-Douglas DC-9-50, 47 DC-9-40, nine DC-9-20, 20 Fokker 50; On order: four Boeing 767-300ER, two 767-200ER, 22 MD-81, 4 MD-82, five MD-83, 4 MD-87.

Singapore Airlines

The flag carrier of Singapore was formed in 1972 when Malaysia-Singapore Airlines was broken up. The joint airline had a short but complex history. In the immediate post-colonial period of the late 1950s Malayan Airways Ltd, with its headquarters in Singapore, was jointly owned by BOAC, Qantas and the newly independent governments of Singapore, Malaya, Sarawak, Brunei and North Borneo. During 1963-66 the carrier operated as Malaysian Airlines; from 1966 to 1971 as Malaysia-Singapore airlines, the consortium was split. Singapore Airlines prospered with the country's newly acquired independence and grew at a phenomenal rate – purchasing Boeing 747-200Bs, Douglas DC-10-30s, Boeing 727-200s and Airbus A300B4s for a growing network of regional routes and long-haul

Left
An unmistakable Airbus A310

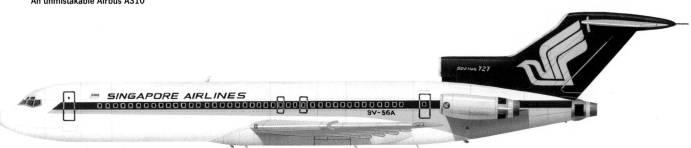

SINGAPORE AIRLINES

9V-SGA

Above
A Boeing 727-200

operations across the Pacific and to Europe. During 1977-79 it operated Concorde on the London – Singapore route via Bahrain in a joint venture with British Airways. As the airline has expanded, the government has adopted a policy of gradually selling its shareholding to local investors.

Singapore Airlines operates scheduled passenger services to 58 cities in 37 countries linking Singapore with Auckland, Christchurch, Adelaide, Brisbane, Darwin, Melbourne, Sydney, Perth, Port Moresby, Denpasar, Jakarta, Medan, Kuala Lumpur, Kuantan, Penang, Langawi, Bangkok, Hong Kong, Taipei, Nagoya, Fukuoka, Osaka, Tokyo, Seoul, Beijing, Shanghai, Manila, Bandar Seri, Begawan, Katmandu, Dhaka, Calcutta, Colombo, Madras, Bombay, New Delhi, Karachi, Malé, Mauritius, Cairo, Dubai, Dharan, Bahrain, Istanbul, Athens, Rome, Vienna, Zurich, Frankfurt, Amsterdam, Paris, Brussels, Copenhagen, London, Manchester, Honolulu, San Francisco, Los Angeles, and Vancouver.

Fleet: seven Airbus A310-300, six A310-200, nine Boeing 747-400, 11 747-300, three 747-300 Combi, five 747-200, one 747-200F. On order 21 747-400, three A310-300, five MD-11.

The flag carrier of South Africa was founded in 1934 as a state-owned enterprise controlled by the SA Railways Administration. The new airline took over the assets and liabilities of the financially struggling Union Airways, which since 1929 had been operating an airmail service between the country's population centers.

South African Airways also took possession of Union's small fleet of Junkers F13s and W34s, with three Ju52/3ms on order. These 14-seaters inaugurated a Johannesberg – Kimberley – Cape Town route on 1 November 1934. New routes were opened as the decade progressed, reaching ever further out across Africa. In 1936 18 ten-seat Junkers Ju 86s went into service. In 1939 28 Lockheed Lodestars were ordered. In 1935 SAA swallowed up the Windhoek-based South West

African Airways, which was also flying a small fleet of Junkers aircraft on mail services around the former German colony.

The war saw SAA's airliners being called up by the government as military transports. In 1944 some of the Lodestars were returned to civil service, to be joined by several DC-4s, DC-3s and Avro Yorks in late 1945.

SAA expanded rapidly after the war. A Johannesburg-London service with three intermediary stops was opened in 1946, while a mixed fleet of DC-3s, Vikings, DH Doves and Lodestars flew a growing internal and regional network. Lockheed Constellations entered service on the airline's long-haul routes in 1950.

When BOAC introduced the DH Comet on the route from London to

Left and above
Boeing 747s began flight service in 1976

Johannesburg in a bid to stay competitive, SAA did a leasing deal to fly the Comets, still in BOAC colors but with SAA crews. After the Comet was grounded following a series of crashes, the Constellations were put back into service. Long-range DC-7Bs supplanted the Lockheed aircraft in 1956, flying the route to London, now with just one intermediary stop at Kano in Nigeria. Technically SAA had already entered the jet age with the Comet 1, but the turbine revolution came in longer lasting form with a fleet of seven Viscount 813s, introduced on the main internal routes in November 1958. Three long-range Boeing 707-344s, special models with full-span leading edge flaps for operations from hot and high-altitude airports, went into service in 1960.

The national government's apartheid policy, meanwhile, made South Africa a pariah in decolonizing black Africa. Overflying rights were progressively denied, but aircraft manufacturers did not hold back from supplying the airline with new equipment. Boeing 727-100s began to replace the Viscounts on the internal routes in 1965. In 1976 the Boeing 747-200 took the airline into the wide-body era, flying from Johannesburg to London following the line of the west African coast in 12 hours. SAA was also a customer for the 747SP or "Special Performance", the very long range version of the airliner which has allowed the airline to beat overflying bans. On a delivery flight a 747SP was flown

from Boeing's Everett plant 10,290 miles non-stop to Cape Town, a record for civil aircraft at the time (1976).

Today SAA flies scheduled passenger and freight services to African destinations including Harare, Gaberone, Moroni, Bulawayo, Windhoek, Maputo, Mauritius, Réunion, Victoria Falls, Lusaka, Lubumbashi and Lilongwe. Long-haul international flights link Johannesburg, Durban and Cape Town with Rio de Janeiro, Hong Kong, Ilha do Sal, Lisbon, Taipei, Rome, Abidjan, Vienna, Zurich, Frankfurt, Paris, Amsterdam, Tel Aviv and London.

Following the gradual dismantling of the apartheid policy, trade and political sanctions are falling away and SAA can look forward to a period of prosperous expansion as trade and travel increase.

Fleet: four Airbus A300B2, four A300B4, one A300C4; two Boeing 747-300, five 747-200B, one 747-200B Combi, five 747SP, 17 Boeing 737-200. On order; seven A320, four 747-400.
Note: SAA operates one restored Ju-52 as a reminder of its historical association with the type.

Swissair

The national airline of Switzerland can trace its ancestry to the pioneering period at the end of World War I when three airlines were founded in short order in 1919 – Mittelholzer based in Zurich, Avion Tourisme in Geneva and the Ad Astra Air Transport Company. This last soon proved to be the dominant force and swallowed the others – using a fleet of Savoia flying boats to offer short hops between the Swiss lakes. Soon after Ad Astra opened an international route from Zurich to Nuremberg in Germany using Junkers F13s.

Meanwhile a rival company, Basle Air Traffic, had begun operations in 1926 using a Dornier Merkur to fly a non-stop service from Zurich to Berlin. Driven by economic expediency, the two companies merged in 1931 as "Swissair" with a fleet of 13 aircraft and an ambitious schedule of European destinations to operate. To replace a rag-bag of aging equipment, first of all Lockheed Orions were acquired in 1932 and then Curtiss Condors in 1934. However a real technical and marketing breakthrough came in 1935 with the first DC-2s offering un-

Above left
A Boeing 747-300

Above
Airbus A310

precedented comfort and efficiency. Their advanced, rubber leading edge de-icing "boots" at last allowed year-round operations, although customers were no doubt more interested in the then highly novel idea of in-flight stewardess service. A direct Zurich-Basle-London route was opened in 1936 in co-operation with Imperial Airways. In 1937 Swissair began to operate the most modern airliner in the world, the Douglas DC-3.

The ubiquitous DC-3 formed the backbone of Swissair's immediate postwar equipment. DC-4s arrived in 1947 and within two years the airline was flying its first transatlantic services. DC-6Bs (for the international routes) and Convair 240s were the backbone of the airline's operations in the early 1950s, to be complemented by DC-7Cs and Convair 440 Metropolitans.

The first jets appeared in 1960 – Caravelles, originally leased from SAS, DC-8-30s and, in 1962, Convair CV990 Coronados for the Far East and South American routes. Douglas DC-9-15s entered service in 1966, soon to be supplanted by the long-nose, "stretched" 32 series as the workhorse of the airline's European network. The first Swissair Boeing 747-200 entered service in 1971, followed a year later by the first of a fleet of DC-10-30s, which replaced the Coronados. In 1978 the first Airbuses were ordered, and the latest type to enter service, in 1991, is the long ranged MD-11.

Today Swissair operates a worldwide network of scheduled passenger and freight services, flying to 68 countries and over 110 cities. The airline has a significant shareholding in Crossair, the Swiss regional carrier, plus holdings in Balair, CTA and various related service and insurance companies.

Fleet: two Boeing 747-357, three 747-357 Combi, five McDonnell Douglas MD-11, seven McDonnell-Douglas DC-10-30, four McDonnell-Douglas DC-10-30ER, five Airbus A310-200, four A310-300, 24 McDonnell-Douglas MD-81, ten Fokker 100; On order, seven Airbus A320, 19 A321, seven McDonnell Douglas MD-11.

Thai International THAI AIRWAYS INTERNATIONAL

The International flag-carrier of Thailand began operations in 1959 with three ex-SAS Douglas DC-6Bs. The Scandinavian airline provided technical and managerial assistance while building up its own hub for Asian services at Bangkok. Flights to Burma, India, Hong Kong and Singapore were begun in 1960.

The Thai government bought out the 15% holding of SAS in 1977. In 1988 the domestic operator, Thai Airways, was merged with the airline. Intercontinental services were launched in 1971 with flights to Australia, followed a year later by services to Europe as Thailand grew in importance as a business and leisure destination. That growth has been reflected in Thai International's modern fleet – with Airbus, Boeing and McDonnell Douglas MD-11 aircraft on order.

Today an extensive network of scheduled passenger services connects Bangkok to 43 destinations in 31 countries throughout the southeast Asia region, the Middle East, Australia, Europe and the US. Thai Airways flies an extensive internal network of domestic services.

Fleet: one MD-11; two Boeing 747-300, six 747-200, three McDonnell Douglas DC-10-30ER; 11 Airbus A300B4, one A300C4 Combi, seven A300-600, two Airbus A310-200, three Boeing 737-200, five BAe146-100/300, one BAe 748, four Shorts 330, two Shorts 360; on order five BAe 146-300, five Airbus A300-600R, three MD-11, six Boeing 747-400, five 737-400, eight A330.

Above
Boeing 747-300

Below
An Airbus A300

Trans World Airlines, one of the most famous names in airline history, was at the end of 1990 struggling for commercial survival as losses mounted once again in a period of worldwide recession in the aircraft industry. In January 1991 American Airlines agreed to buy TWA's routes from the US to London, Gatwick, in a cash-raising bid, a move which precipitated a bitter Anglo-US battle over rights to fly from Heathrow.

The airline was formed on 1 October 1930 as Transcontinental and Western Air, the result of a merger between Transcontinental Air Trans-

port, a part of Western Air Express (the other part became Western Airlines) and Pittsburgh Aviation Industries Corporation. The new company had a key contract – to fly air mail on a central multi-stop trans-America route from New York to Los Angeles, which effectively subsidized the passenger operation. Locked out of the production run for rival United Airline's Boeing 247, the airline commissioned a new transport aircraft from Douglas which emerged in July 1933 as the single prototype Douglas DC-1 in TWA markings. The first of 20 follow-on DC-2s was delivered in mid-1934. The DC-2s were able to make the

continued

transcontinental mail flights in 18 hours.

The larger DC-3 joined the TWA fleet in 1936, followed by the first of five Boeing Model 307 Stratoliners in 1940. In 1939 Howard Hughes bought a large block of the company's stock. The mercurial millionaire pressed for a long-range luxurious aircraft that would eventually emerge as the Constellation (it entered service in 1944) and provoked some heated boardroom dramas. The war meant that TWA's operations were largely militarized – including a transatlantic air bridge flown by the Stratoliners.

During the postwar air travel boom TWA opened intercontinental routes via Gander and Shannon to London and Paris and to North Africa. A Constellation-flown route onwards from western Europe to China was opened in 1948 via Athens, Cairo, Dharan, Bombay and Colombo to Hanoi, Canton and Shanghai. Financial and industrial problems at the end of the 1940s, including a prolonged pilot's strike in 1946, slowed down the company's growth. But in 1950 the carrier officially retitled itself Trans World Airways and began a new period of confident expansion. It ordered a fleet of Martin 4-0-4s for its internal routes and Super Constellations for the long-haul routes. The last DC-3 was retired by 1953. However, boardroom battles with the increasingly eccentric Howard Hughes began to dominate the management's atten-

tion from the mid-1950s onwards. Hughes was forced to surrender his voting power to a committee of trustees. In 1961 a damages suit was filed against him for breaches of anti-trust laws in the monopolizing supply of equipment and finance. This legal battle did not end until 1968 when the court found in the airline's favor. Hughes by this time had become a complete recluse.

TWA had managed meanwhile to get into the jet age early. Its first Boeing 707-131 entered service on 20 March 1959, flying non-stop from San Francisco to New York. In 1961 the Convair 880 was introduced on domestic routes – this aircraft was built to Howard Hughes' own specification.

In 1964 Boeing 727s began operations on domestic services, followed by DC-9s. The last TWA Constellation scheduled passenger service was flown in 1967, into Kansas City. TWA's management toyed with the ideas of ordering either a US-built supersonic transport or the Anglo-French Concorde but recoiled from trying to make SST operations a commercial reality without massive government subsidies. In 1971 TWA entered the wide-body era with its first Boeing 747-100s, Lockheed L-1011 TriStars following in 1972.

On 26 September 1985 TWA was taken over by the Wall Street entrepreneur Carl Icahn, who acquired 52% of the company's shares. The company has been in and out of profit since the takeover but has not been able to substantially modernize its aging fleet. The company took over the St Louis-based Ozark Air Lines in 1987.

The airline's route network connects over 100 destinations within the US, with the airline's main hubs at St Louis and New York, JFK. Transatlantic services are operated to the major cities of western Europe.

Fleet: 14 Boeing 747-100, five 747-200B, 14 Lockheed L-1011 TriStar 1, eight TriStar 50, 11 TriStar 100, ten Boeing 767-200ER, one 767-200, 56 Boeing 727-200, 18 727-100, 25 MD-82, four MD-83, three McDonnell-Douglas DC-9-40, 36 DC-9-30, one DC-9-30F, five DC-9-15; On order; 20 Airbus A330-300.

Page 105
Lockheed L-1011 TriStar
Above left
A McDonnell Douglas MD-80
Left
Tailfin of Boeing 747
Above
A Boeing 747

United Airlines

United Airlines was formed on 27 March 1931 when four pioneer airlines came together under the single management umbrella of the ambitious United Aircraft and Transport Company (UA&T). They were Boeing Air Transport, Pacific Air Transport, National Air Transport and Varney Airlines.

National had been formed in 1925 to fly air mail from Chicago via Kansas City to Dallas and later from New York to Chicago. Varney had been founded a year later as an air taxi and flying school. Soon it, too, had a vital air mail contract. Pacific started flying mail from Seattle to Los Angeles at the same time. Boeing Air Transport, an offshoot of the aircraft manufacturing business, also made a successful bid to fly mail — between San Francisco and Chicago. Boeing produced the advanced Model 247 all-metal monoplane in 1933, putting UA&T in a commanding technical lead over its competitors, until they turned to

Left
Boeing 737-300

Above
Boeing 727-200

Douglas. TWA got the DC-2 into service in 1934; American was flying the world-beating DC-3 a year later. An Act of Congress forbade the grouping of manufacturers and airlines within the same company and so United Airlines came into being as a separate entity in 1934, divorcing itself from Boeing.

The Air Mail Act of 1934 broke up the cosy monopoly of air mail routes awarded four years earlier and United had to fend for itself much more. The airline led its marketing offensive with trained nurses recruited as stewardesses and introduced galley-cooked in-flight meals and sleeper accommodation in 1936.

Half of United's fleet was called up for war work during 1942-45. DC-3s and DC-4s were used to get the airline back into civil operations, followed by Boeing 377 Stratoliners, DC-6s and DC-7s. The first overseas route, to Hawaii, began in 1946. As the jet age dawned the airline briefly considered buying DH Comets but ordered DC-8s instead. The Douglas jet transports entered service in 1959, the year United took over Capital Airlines with a fleet of turboprop Viscounts. Controversially, United ordered French-built Caravelles as its first medium-range jets (the only US customer for this aircraft), later supplanted by 727s. The first wide-body 747s were ordered in 1966. In 1986 United took over Pan Am's Pacific routes, and in early 1991 also took over Pan Am's

transatlantic operations from London (Heathrow). At the end of 1990, United was the launch customer for the new Boeing 777 widebody twinjet, placing an order for no less than 34 aircraft.

Today the airline operates from five major hubs at Washington, Chicago, Denver, San Francisco and Narita (Tokyo). United flies a large network of scheduled passenger services, linking 154 destination in the US, Canada and Mexico with international services to the Far East, Australia and New Zealand.

Fleet: eight Boeing 747-400, two 747-200B, 18 747-100, 11 747SP, 19 Boeing 767-200, 12 757-200, four 737-500, 101 737-300, 74 737-200, 104 Boeing 727-200, 36 727-100, 46 McDonnell-Douglas DC-10-10, 8 DC-10-30, 21 DC-8-71; On order, 34 Boeing 777, 16 767-300ER, 66 757-200, 37 747-400, 124 B737-300/400/500.

US Air

↑ 23 · 32 →

This major US airline is the successor to several famous names in American domestic civil aviation. It is the lineal descendant of Allegheny Airlines (itself the scion of All American Airways), which was formed in 1953 to operate commuter services in the US eastern corridor. Indianapolis-based Lake Central was taken over in 1969, New York based Mohawk Airlines (formerly Robinson Airlines) in 1972.

However, the acquisition which really catapulted US Air into the big league was the take over of the North Carolina based Piedmont in 1986. Piedmont Aviation was formed in 1940 and gained airline status

in 1948. By 1986 it had grown to operate a fleet of 177 modern aircraft, employed a staff of 22,000 and flew 22.8 million passengers a year from 92 airports. By comparison US Air in 1986 had a fleet of around 120 aircraft and a staff of 13,000. The integration was completed by 1989 with all aircraft and services operated under US Airs colours and the airline now ranks Number 3 among the US major airlines in terms of passengers carried. USAir Group, the airline's parent company also owns four major regional US commuter airlines, Henson, Jetstream, Pennsylvania Airlines and Allegheny Commuter.

Fleet: nine Boeing 767-200, 44 Boeing 737-400, 80 Boeing 737-200, 102 Boeing 7377-300, 29 Boeing 727-200, 74 McDonnell Douglas DC-9-30, 19 McDonnell Douglas MD-81, 12 McDonnell Douglas MD-82; 18 BAe 146-200; 25 Fokker F28-4000, 20 Fokker F28-1000, 24 Fokker 100; On order 10 Boeing 737-300, 24 Boeing 737-400; 16 Fokker 100

Note: BAe. 146s currently withdrawn from service.

Above
A Fokker 100, one of 24 in the current fleet

Aerolíneas Argentinas

Created in 1949 when several independent operators were merged, the new airline operated a fleet of DC-3s, DC-4s and DC-6s, several Convair CV 240s and six Sandringham flying boats.

The first jets, Comet 4Cs, were ordered in 1958 in a move designed to keep the airline competitive with BOAC. Caravelles arrived in 1960 and turboprop HS 748s in 1962. Boeing 707s replaced the Comets in 1966, Boeing 737s appeared in the fleet in 1969 and Boeing 747-200Bs in 1976.

The airline's route network covers the whole of the Americas and stretches across the Pacific and South Pole to New Zealand, Australia and the Far East, and across the Atlantic to Europe and South Africa.
Fleet: six Boeing 747-200B, one 747SP, one Boeing 707-320B, eight Boeing 727-200, nine Boeing 737-200, two 737-200C; three Fokker F28-100, one Fokker F28-4000

AeroMexico

This airline, originally known as Aeronaves de Mexico, began flights between Mexico City and Acapulco in September 1934. In the 1950s several smaller operations were swallowed up and in 1959 the airline was nationalized and the stake held by Pan Am was bought by the government. The airline, although state-owned, was declared bankrupt in 1988. After restructuring a 65% stake was sold to a banking consortium, the rest going to the Mexican pilots' union. The airline was renamed Aerovías de Mexico but still is marketed as AeroMexico. Privatization was commercially successful and the airline was back in profit in 1990. From Mexico City 35 domestic destinations are served, plus five US cities.
Fleet: three McDonnell Douglas DC-10-30, two DC-10-15, eight MD-82, 16 DC-9-30, five MD-88. On order five McDonnell Douglas MD-88

Air Afrique

This airline was set up in 1961 as a joint venture by 11 newly independent former French African colonies, each with a 6% interest. Air France and UAT each held a 17% interest through a controlling body called Sodetraf.

Ownership has been somewhat redistributed with the withdrawal of Cameroon and Gabon and the entry of Benin and Togo into the consortium. Each member owns 7%, the remainder belonging still to Sodetraf. The company's administrative headquarters are at Abidjan, capital of the Ivory Coast.

An extensive route network is flown within Francophone Africa and to Paris, London and Frankfurt, New York and Jeddah.

Fleet: three Airbus A300B4; one McDonnell Douglas DC-8-63F, three McDonnell Douglas DC-10-30 (plus other aircraft on short term lease): On order, 5 Airbus A310-300.

Air Algérie

The original Air Algérie was founded in the former French colony in 1949. In 1953 it merged with the Compagnie Air Transport to form the present operation, which became the national carrier in 1962 after independence. Initial equipment included Constellations, DC-4s and Caravelles. The airline was nationalized in 1972. As well as providing a comprehensive domestic network, Air Algérie flies scheduled passenger and cargo services to 34 international destinations in North and West Africa, Europe and the Middle East.

Fleet: two Airbus A310-200; two Boeing 767-300, 10 Boeing 727-200, 16 Boeing 737-200C (including three cargo variants); eight Fokker F27-400; three Lockheed L-100-30

Air BC

This British Columbia-based airline was founded in 1980 through the merger of a number of small regional operators. Today it flies a fleet of BAe 146s and twin-props on regional and commuter services in western Canada and to Portland in the US, with its main operating hub at Vancouver where it operates as an "Air Canada Connector". The international airline acquired a 75% holding in Air BC in 1987.
Fleet: five BAe 146, six BAe Jetstream 31; four Boeing Canada Dash 7, 16 Dash 8; eight DHC Twin Otter

Air Jamaica

Founded in 1968 with technical and financial assistance from Air Canada, Jamaica's flag carrier became fully state-owned in 1980. Scheduled passenger services connect Kingston and Montego Bay with destinations in the Caribbean, and with Miami, New York, Philadelphia, Baltimore, Atlanta, Los Angeles, Toronto and Tampa. Direct services to London are operated jointly with British Airways, using BA aircraft.
Fleet: four Airbus A300B4; four Boeing 727-200

Air Lanka

The national airline of Sri Lanka succeeded Air Ceylon in 1979. Air Ceylon had been formed by the government in 1947, soon after independence, sharing ownership with KLM who provided technical assistance in operating a small fleet of DC-3s and two DC-4s. The partnership with KLM ended in 1961, but jet services to London began in 1962 in conjunction with BOAC using Comet 4s and, later, VC-10s. In 1979 the new Air Lanka leased two Boeing 707s, which were eventually replaced by the current Lockheed TriStars, the first of which entered service in 1980. During the mid-1980s traffic was badly hit by terrorist activity, which included the destruction of a TriStar.

Today, scheduled passenger and freight services are flown from Colombo to various destinations in Asia and Europe.

Fleet: three Lockheed L-1011-500, two Lockheed L-1011-100, one Boeing 737-200: On order, 1 Airbus A320

Air Malta

The national airline of Malta was formed in 1974 and is now a major holding company for leisure and hotel interests on the island. The operation is 96.4% government-owned. Scheduled passenger and cargo services are operated to the capitals of western Europe and to Cairo, Benghazi and Tripoli. A Boeing 767 was to be leased in 1991 for a new service to Australia via Bangkok.

Fleet: one Airbus A320-200, six Boeing 737-200. On order one Airbus A320; three Boeing 737-500

Air Mauritius

The national carrier of the Indian Ocean state of Mauritius was founded in 1967 and for ten years international services were operated in conjunction with Air France, British Airways and Air India. In 1977 the airline undertook responsibility for its own operations but the founders still hold small stakes, the Mauritian government having a 51% controlling interest. Local services are operated to the nearby small island of Rodrigues. There are regional links with Reunion, Antananarivo and Nairobi, and long-haul services to Bombay, Hong Kong, Kuala Lumpur, Singapore, Durban, Johannesburg, Harare, Rome, Geneva, Paris, London, Zurich and Frankfurt.
Fleet: two Boeing 747SP, two Boeing 767-200ER; one DHC Twin Otter; two Bell JetRanger; one ATR 42. On order one ATR 42

Air Pacific

The national airline of Fiji has operated under this name since 1971. Before then it was known as Fiji Airways, established in 1948 in a joint agreement between British Overseas Airways Corporation, Qantas and the New Zealand operator, TEAL. In 1990 Qantas sold its stake in the profitable airline to the Fiji government. Other stakes are held by the governments of Tonga, Nauru, Kiribati and Western Samoa. Services are operated between the Fijian capital, Suva, and major Australian cities, and to Tokyo, Tonga, Western Samoa, Vanuatu and Honiara.
Fleet: one Boeing 747-200 (leased), one Boeing 767-200ER; two ATR42-300. On order one Boeing 767-300ER

Air UK

This independent British airline is the heir to many famous names in the postwar history of British civil aviation. Air UK itself was formed in 1980 on the merger of British Island Airways, Air West, Air Anglia and Air Wales. BIA was the successor to Jersey Airlines, Manx Airlines and Silver City Airways. In 1988 the airline took over British Airway's Gatwick to Edinburgh and Glasgow routes. Major British cities and the Channel Islands are served from Heathrow, Gatwick and Stansted. European destinations served are Amsterdam, Bergen, Brussels, Paris, Stavanger and Zurich. The holiday charter operation, Air UK Leisure, is a sister company.

Air UK's headquarters is now at Stansted, from where a substantial network of scheduled services is operated.

Fleet (Air UK): six BAe 146-300, four 146-200, two 146-100; one Fokker F27-600, two F27-500, 11 F27-200, one F27-100; two Shorts 360. On order five BAe 146

Fleet (Air UK Leisure): 4 Boeing 737-400; On Order, 3 737-400

Alaska Airlines

Originally founded as McGee Airways in 1932, this airline, based in Seattle, Washington, is now a major carrier along the US west coast.

The postwar fleet consisted of Curtiss C-46s and DC-4s, DC-6s being introduced in the early 1950s and the first jets, in the shape of Convair 880s, in 1962.

The airline has continued to grow. It services 36 destinations and has joint marketing agreements with Horizon Air and American Airlines, providing through services from Anchorage and Fairbanks in Alaska to Chicago, Dallas/Fort Worth, Houston and Washington DC. This gives a total of over 90 destinations in all.

Fleet: one Boeing 727-100, 26 727-200, seven Boeing 737-200C; 28 McDonnell Douglas MD-82/83. On order, 6 MD-83, 20 MD-90; 20 Boeing 737-400.

Aloha Airlines

This Hawaii-based inter-island airline began life as Trans-Pacific in 1946, adopting its present name in 1958. Operations began with a fleet of ubiquitous DC-3s. Fokker F27 turboprop services were started in 1960. Now the fleet is all Boeing 737. Passenger, freight and parcel services are run between Lihue, Honolulu, Kahului, Kona and Hilo. Fleet: nine Boeing 737-200, four 737-200QC, two 737-300 (plus three 737 on lease). On order, four Boeing 737-300

Ansett Australia

This Melbourne-based major Australian domestic carrier traces its roots to Ansett Airways founded in 1936 by Reginald M.Ansett with a single Fokker Universal. In 1957 it took over Australian National Airways (ANA), bringing in new equipment such as Viscounts and Electras. Ansett grew quickly by swallowing more companies. The first jets came in 1964 – Boeing 727s, followed by DC-9s in 1967. Rapid growth continued through the 1970s. In 1980 the holding company, Ansett Transport Industries (ATI), was bought out by a consortium led by the TNT transport group and Rupert Murdoch's News Corporation. Scheduled services are flown on a network covering the whole of Australia.
Fleet: eight Airbus A320; five Boeing 767-200, five Boeing 727-200, one 727-200F, 15 Boeing 737-300; two Fokker F27, ten Fokker 50. On order, four Airbus A320, ten A321-100.

Asiana Airlines

Matching the explosive growth of the South Korean economy, Asiana has grown to major airline status in less than three years. Formed in 1988 as a subsidiary of the Kumho Group, an industrial conglomerate, the airline now operates 84 domestic flights per day and 70 flights per week on an international network that includes destinations such as Taipei, Hong Kong, Bangkok, Singapore, Tokyo and Nagoya. At the end of 1991 a service to Los Angeles will commence using Boeing 747-400 Combis and New York and Honolulu will also be included when aircraft are available. Asiana is not permitted to serve Europe, the Middle East or Australia as these routes are reserved for Korean Air.

The airline's policy of operating all new aircraft is confirmed by large orders for Boeing 747s and 767s to supplement the existing fleet. Fleet: ten 737-400, two 737-500, two 767-300. On order: 13 737-400, 11 747-400, 12 767-300.

Australian Airlines

The state-owned domestic airline was founded in 1946 as Trans-Australia Airlines. The present name was adopted in 1986. In 1988 it changed its status from a statutory corporation to a public limited company in preparation for privatization and the de-regulation of the Australian airline industry.

Fleet: five Airbus A300B4; 16 Boeing 737-300, six 737-400, nine Boeing 727-200, one 727-100C; four Boeing Canada Dash 8; two Fokker F27-600. On order 12 Boeing 737-400

Austrian Airlines

Formed in 1957 with the help of SAS and a consortium of Austrian banks, this airline began operating with four chartered Viscounts. Today the airline operates major international routes to 56 cities in 36 countries in Europe, North Africa, the Middle East and Japan. A Vienna-Moscow-Tokyo service is jointly operated with Aeroflot and All Nippon Airways. Austrian also flies an extensive network of charters through its 80%-owned subsidiary, Austrian Air Transport. Internal and commuter flights are flown by the wholly-owned subsidiary, Austrian Air Services, using a fleet of Fokker 50s. Austrian is 61% owned by the government, 8% by Swissair, 3.5% by All Nippon and 1.5% by Air France.
Fleet: two Airbus A310-324; five Fokker 50; eight McDonnell Douglas MD-81, six MD-82, five MD-87. On order two Airbus A310-324, six Airbus A320, seven Airbus A321; two McDonnell Douglas MD-83; one Fokker 50

Aviaco

Aviación y Comercio

Founded in 1948 in Bilbao as a cargo airline with a fleet of three Bristol Freighters, this Spanish domestic carrier began to offer scheduled passenger services in the 1950s – across Spain and to the Balearics – with a fleet of DC-3s, DH Herons and Sud-Est Languedocs. Holiday charters also brought important business. Today the airline is Spain's major domestic carrier and a subsidiary of Iberia. From the Madrid hub services are flown to Valencia, Murcia, Málaga, Jérez, Badajoz, Vigo, Valladolid, La Coruña, Santander, Granada, Almería, Bilbao, San Sebastian, Pamplona, Reus, Zaragoza, Ibiza, Palma and Mahon.
Fleet: eight Fokker F27-600; five McDonnell Douglas MD-83, 23 McDonnell Douglas DC-9-30. On order 13 McDonnell Douglas MD-88 (deliveries began in 1991)

Avianca

The national carrier of Colombia has its roots in the oldest airline in the Americas, SCADTA, founded in 1919 by German investors. In 1940 this operation merged with Servicio Aéreo Colombiano, founded in 1931, and with 80% backing from Pan American to form Avianca. The last shares owned by Pan Am in the company were acquired in 1978. Bogotá is the hub of an extensive domestic network. International services are flown to major South American cities, to the Caribbean, Miami, New York and Los Angeles, and to Madrid, Paris and Frankfurt.

Fleet: one Boeing 747-200 Combi, three Boeing 707-320B, seven Boeing 727-200, eleven 727-100, two Boeing 767-200ER

Aviogenex

This state-owned Yugoslav air charter company operates holiday and leisure flights in conjunction with Yugotours. It was founded as Genex Airlines in 1968 and is currently based at Belgrade, employing some 400 staff. In common with many east european airlines it has gradually replaced its soviet built aircraft with more competitive western aircraft and four remaining Tu-134s have been withdrawn from service. The recent civil unrest in Yugoslavia has caused the virtual cessation of holiday charter traffic and this will undoubtedly affect future plans. Fleet: four Boeing 727-200, four Boeing 737-200.

Bangladesh Biman

A national airline was formed in 1972 soon after the creation of the new state of Bangladesh from what had been East Pakistan. Domestic services link the capital Dhaka with Chittagong, Cox's Bazar, Sylhet, Jessore, Ishurdi and Saidpur. International services are flown to London, Amsterdam, Rome, Athens, Singapore, Kuala Lumpur, Bangkok, Rangoon, Katmandu, Calcutta, Bombay, Karachi, Dubai, Abu Dhabi, Muscat, Doha, Dharan, Jeddah and Tripoli.
Fleet: four DC-10-30; two Fokker F28-4000; two BAe ATP. On order 1 BAe ATP

Birmingham European Airways

This small business-orientated airline was founded in 1983 as Birmingham Executive Airways. It was acquired by the Plimsoll Line shipping group in 1988 when the name was changed to its present form. British Airways are a major stakeholder and there is a close integration of services between the two carriers at Birmingham where the new Eurohub terminal enables rapid transfers between flights. BEA upgraded to jets in 1990 when several ex-British Airways BAC-111s replaced turboprops on most European routes.

Scheduled passenger services are flown from its operating hub at Birmingham International Airport to Amsterdam, Belfast, Copenhagen, Frankfurt, Milan, Oslo, Newcastle, Stuttgart and Cork. Closely allied to British Airways, BEA flies several services for the flag carrier.
Fleet: five BAe One-Eleven 400; two Shorts 360, three Gulfstream 1, three Jetstream 31.

Braathens SAFE

This independent Norwegian airline was founded after World War II as a subsidiary of Braathens shipping line. Early equipment included DC-3s and DC-4s, and a service was operated to Hong Kong during 1949-54 — hence the initials, which stood for South American and Far East air transport. Today a small, modern fleet operates a network of scheduled domestic services within Norway and, in addition, a service to the island of Spitsbergen above the Arctic Circle from Bergen and Tromsö. The airline is the launch customer for the Boeing 737-500. Holiday charters provide important business in the summer. The Busy Bee charter operation, a wholly owned subsidiary, is, together with Braathen Helicopter, active in the North Sea oilfields. In 1991 Braathens began scheduled services to the UK and Denmark.

Fleet: fourteen Boeing 737-200, five 737-400, three 737-500. On order: one Boeing 737-400, 17 737-500

Britannia Airways

The Luton-based Britannia has become the largest charter company in the world. Originally founded in 1962 as Euravia, in 1964 it began operating the big turboprop Bristol Britannia and changed its name. A year later it was acquired by the Canadian-based Thomson Organization. In 1988 Thomson bought the Horizon Travel business and merged its airline, Orion, with Britannia. Although hit by a profits slump in 1990, Britannia is replacing its aging 737-200 fleet, with orders for up to 20 150-seaters expected in 1992. Britannia operates charter flights from the UK to Mediterranean holiday destinations and long-haul services to Australia, the Caribbean and the US. Scheduled flights are also operated to European resorts and from Luton to Belfast.

Fleet: three Boeing 767-200, six Boeing 767-200ER, four Boeing 757 (leased), 23 Boeing 737-200, six 737-300. On order six Boeing 767-200ER, six Boeing 757-200

British Midland

Derbyshire-based British Midland traces its parentage to Derby Aviation founded in 1938. In 1953 Derby Airways began flying domestic services in the UK with a fleet of six DC-3s. In 1964 the name British Midland was adopted and a series of changes of ownership followed. In 1978 came a management buy-out and the airline has successfully expanded its activities and revenues since then, through internal growth and takeovers. Manx Airlines is a subsidiary, as is Loganair Airways through the holding company, Airlines of Britain Holdings plc, formed in 1987. SAS acquired 24.9% of the company at the end of 1988. British Midland currently operates a comprehensive scheduled services network.
Fleet: three Boeing 737-400, six 737-300; eight McDonnell Douglas DC-9-32, six DC-9-15; two Boeing Canada Dash 7; three BAe ATP.

BWIA

Trinidad and Tobago Airways was formed on 1 January 1980, through the merger of British West Indian Airways International and Trinidad and Tobago Air Services (TTAS). BWIA was a Caribbean regional operator under BOAC's control, providing services all over the West Indies and to Miami , New York and London. By the late 1950s the local fleet consisted of Viscount 702s and 772 Series, plus three DC-3s. The long-haul fleet was made up of Britannias and crews leased from BOAC. In November 1961 the Trinidad government acquired a 90% holding, acquiring the remainder in 1967. TTAS, formed in June 1974 by the government, operated high-frequency shuttle flights linking the islands of Trinidad and Tobago.

BWIA operates between the Caribbean, US and Europe.
Fleet: one McDonnell Douglas DC-9-51, nine McDonnell Douglas MD-83, Four Lockheed L-1011 Tristar 500.

Cameroon Airlines

Formed in 1971 when the Cameroon government pulled out of Air Afrique, this national airline is still owned in part (25%) by Air France. The rest is owned by the government of this former French West African Territory. From the capital, Douala, the airline operates an extensive Domestic network and international services to African capitals and to London, Paris, Rome, Zurich, Geneva and Frankfurt.

Fleet: one Boeing 747-200B Combi (leased), one Boeing 737-200, two 737-200C; two BAe 748

CrossAir

This Swiss regional airline was founded in 1975, but scheduled passenger services did not begin until 2 July 1979, using Saab 340 regional twin-props. Today the airline, 38% of which is owned by Swissair, operates an extensive passenger network throughout western Europe. It has recently acquired a 35% share in the Czechoslovakia-based Tatra Air, which will fly a Saab 340 between Bratislava, Zurich and Munich.

Fleet: three BAe 146-200; 24 Saab 340, four Fokker 50. On order five BAe 146-200; 25 Saab 2000, one Fokker 50.

Cruzeiro

One of the pioneering airlines of South America, the Rio de Janeiro-based Cruzeiro was founded in 1927 by German entrepreneurs as the Condor Syndikat. It became Serviços Aéreos Condor in 1941, backed by Brazilian private capital. In January 1943 it was nationalized as Serviços Aéreos Cruzeiro do Sul. After World War II a large fleet of DC-3s, Convair 440s and Fairchild C-82 freighters was operated on domestic services and to regional capitals. In 1975 control was bought by the owners of the rival airline, Varig, and flight schedules were integrated.The airline operates a large network of scheduled passenger services within Brazil and to the capitals of Bolivia, Uruguay and Argentina.

Fleet: two Airbus A300B4; six Boeing 727-100, six Boeing 737-200

CSA

The national airline of Czechoslovakia resumed operations in 1945 with a handful of war-weary DC-3s and Junkers Ju-52/3m trimotors. Civil air operations had begun in the central European country with the founding of CSA in 1923. Four years later the privately owned Ceskoslovensko Letecka Spolecnost (CLS) was formed and it was what remained of these airlines after the war that were merged following the liberation.

After the Communist takeover in 1948 the airline was nationalized and re-equipped with Soviet aircraft. Ilyushin-designed Il-14s, built under license by Avia, formed the bulk of the early equipment. Operations with Tu-104 jets began in 1957 and turboprop Ilyushin Il-18s were introduced in 1960.

Fleet: two Airbus A310-300, nine Ilyushin Il-62, two Il-18, seven Tupolev Tu-154M, seven Tu-134A, six Yakovlev Yak-40; On order two Tu-154M

Cyprus Airways

Cyprus Airways Ltd was founded in 1947 by the local government of Cyprus, local business interests and BEA with a 22% holding. The airline originally operated a small fleet of DC-3s but in 1958 arrangements were made for the airline's operations, which were principally in the Mediterranean area, to be flown by BEA Viscounts and Comet 4Bs. In 1974 the airline's entire fleet (four Tridents and a BAC One-Eleven) was lost during the Turkish occupation of the northern part of the island. Today the airline is 84% owned by the Cyprus government, and scheduled passenger and freight services link the island with Athens, Thessaloniki, Rhodes, London, Paris, Manchester, Birmingham, Frankfurt, Munich, Zurich, Geneva, Cairo, Damascus, Tel Aviv, Jeddah, Riyadh, Bahrain, Amman and Dubai. A new livery was introduced in 1991. Fleet: four Airbus A310-200, four Airbus A320-200; three British Aerospace One-Eleven 500. On order four Airbus A320-200

Dan Air

Dan-Air is still better known as a holiday charter company than as a scheduled airline – although by 1990 it had become the UK's second largest scheduled carrier to international destinations. Dan Air was formed in 1953 as a subsidiary of the shipping brokers, Davies and Newman Holdings, from where the name is derived. In its early years local services were flown to France and the Channel Islands using Airspeed Elizabethans, DC-3s and Doves, while Avro Yorks flew freighting contracts. Today scheduled passenger flights depart from British airports to holiday and business destinations all over western Europe.

Fleet: one Airbus A300B4; ten Boeing 727-200, one 727-100 (for disposal), three 737-400, two 737-300, four 737-200; 11 BAe One-Eleven 500, one One-Eleven 300, two One-Eleven 200, two BAe 146-300, two BAe 146-100, six BAe 748 (for disposal); On order, three 737-300, two 737-400

DAN-AIR LONDON

G-BKMN

DLT

Deutsche Luftverkehrgesellschaft or DLT is a major German domestic operator, 52% owned by the national carrier, Lufthansa. It was founded in 1958 as Ostfriesische Lufttaxi, adopting its present name in 1974. The airline operates joint ticketing and scheduling arrangements with Lufthansa, serving destinations across the newly united country and using its twin-prop fleet as feeders. DLT also makes its own international flights to European centers from Cologne, Munich, Hamburg and Frankfurt.

Fleet: seventeen Fokker 50; On order, 13 Canadair Regional Jets, three Fokker 50.

Note; DLTs fleet of 12 EMB120 Brasilias is currently leased to Midway Express.

Dominicana

The airline of the Dominican Republic, Compañia Dominicana de Aviación, C por A, was founded in 1944 by a cartel of local businessmen with a 40% holding by Pan Am. Early equipment included DC-3s, DC-4s and Curtiss C-46s flying to Haiti and Miami. Today it is wholly state-owned and scheduled passenger services are flown to Curaçao, Caracas, Port-au-Prince, Aruba, Miami, San Juan, and New York. The Spanish airline, Iberia, was approached, with a view to taking a 40% shareholding in order to overcome financial problems.

Fleet: one Boeing 707-320C, one Boeing 727-200, one 727-100, one 727-100C

Dragonair

A dynamic, semi-independent regional airline, Hong Kong Dragon Airlines, or Dragonair, was founded by Macau- and Hong Kong-based business interests in 1985, with a network of routes into southern and eastern China. In early 1990 sizeable shareholdings were sold to the Swire Group (owners of Cathay Pacific) and to the International Trust and Investment Corporation of China. The airline flies direct to eight regional cities of the People's Republic and to Beijing and Shanghai. Services to Beijing are flown in Cathay-liveried TriStars. Scheduled passenger services are also flown to the Thai resorts of Phuket and Pattaya, Kagishima, Dhaka and Katmandu.

Fleet: five Boeing 737-200; one Lockheed Tristar (leased)

East West Airlines

This Australian domestic carrier was founded in 1947, with four DC-3s flying between Brisbane and Sydney and points in New South Wales and southern Queensland. The company was taken over by Rupert Murdoch's News Corporation and the TNT transport group in 1987. Today East West operates scheduled passenger services to major cities and to leisure and holiday destinations, including Mount Isa, Ayers Rock, Canberra, Brisbane, Melbourne, Sydney, Ayers Rock, Hobart and Norfolk Island. The current F28 fleet is being replaced by the BAe 146.

Fleet: four Fokker F28; five BAe 146-300. On order three BAe 146-300

Ecuatoriana

An airline was formed in Ecuador in 1947, the Compañía Ecuatoriana de Aviación (CEA) SA, flying two war-weary C-46s on a route between Miami and Santiago, Chile, stopping at Panama, the capital, Quito, Guayaquil and Lima along the way. The present company took over the operating rights and assets of CEA in 1974. A small fleet links Quito and Guayaquil to New York, Los Angeles, Chicago, Mexico City and other capitals in Latin America. An all-cargo service is flown to New York, Panama City and Miami. Contract technical support is provided by Israeli Aircraft Industries. The airline's recent order for two leased Airbus A310 means that Ecuatoriana will be the first South American operator of this type.
Fleet: three Boeing 707-320B, one 707-320C; one McDonnell Douglas DC-10-30. On order two Airbus A310-300

Emirates

Formed as the national airline of the United Arab Emirates (UAE) in 1985, on the initiative of the government of Dubai, Emirates has quickly won an international reputation for service and efficiency with a modern Airbus-based fleet. Scheduled passenger services are flown from Dubai to Amman, Bandar Abbas, Bombay, Cairo, Colombo, Damascus, Delhi, Dhaka, Frankfurt, Istanbul, Jeddah, Karachi, Kuwait (until the invasion of August 1990), London and the Maldives.
Fleet: three Airbus A300-600R, two Airbus A310-300; three Boeing 727-200. On order, one Airbus A300-600R, three Airbus A310-300 (options for 2 MD-11 and 2 Airbus A330)

Ethiopian Airlines

When this was founded in 1946, initial support came from TWA, with aircraft drawn largely from the TWA fleet, including DC-6Bs and DC-3s serving a largely domestic route network. Today the airline of this troubled country manages to operate scheduled passenger services to 40 domestic destinations. Intra-African services are operated from the capital, Addis Ababa, to Abijdan, Abu Dhabi, Accra, Aden, Bamako, Brazzaville, Conakry, Dakar, Djibouti, Harare, Niamey, Sana'a, Nairobi, Entebbe, Dar-es-Salaam, Kilimanjiro, Lomé, Kinshasa, Douala, Lagos, Monrovia, Luanda, Khartoum, Jeddah and Cairo. There are also some international services.

Fleet: three Boeing 767-200ER, one Boeing 757PF, one Boeing 757-200, one Boeing 707-320C, four Boeing 727-200, one Boeing 737-200; six Douglas DC-3, six DHC Twin Otter; On order, three Boeing 757-200

FAT

This Taiwan domestic airline began charter operations in 1957, starting scheduled passenger services in 1965. Today routes are flown from the capital, Taipei, to Kaoisung, Hualien, Tainan and Makung. International charters are also flown.

Fleet: six Boeing 737-200, one 737-100. On order two ATR72

Federal Express

The largest air freight carrier in the world, Fedex is a public corporation, founded in 1971. It specializes in door-to-door collection and delivery of parcels and packages and offers a range of ranked-priority services. The operational center is at Memphis International Airport, Tennessee, from where loads are despatched every night all over the US. Operations began in 1973 with a small fleet of Falcon 20 biz-jets. Deregulation of the US air cargo industry in 1977 allowed long-range services to be opened up. A British subsidiary was acquired in 1986 and London and Brussels sorting centers were opened. In 1989 the California-based Flying Tiger Line was acquired with its fleet of Boeing 747 freighters

and extensive air cargo operations in the Pacific rim, Asia and Latin America.
Fleet: 149 Boeing 727-100/200, 16 Boeing 747-100F/200F, 27 McDonnell Douglas DC-10, two DC-8-73F; 26 Fokker F27-500/600; 148 Cessna 208 Caravans. On order eight McDonnell Douglas MD-11F (plus 11 options), 25 Airbus A300-600F (plus 50 options)

Finnair

Finnair was founded as the private company ''Aero O/Y'' in 1923, using a fleet of Junkers floatplanes to provide services from Baltic harbors until airports began to be built in Finland in the mid-1930s. Operations began again after World War II with a handful of DC-3s. Convair 340s were introduced in 1953 and a service to Moscow from Helsinki was opened in 1956. The first jets, Caravelles, entered service in 1960, and for intercontinental routes two DC-8-62 arrived in 1969.

Finnair was the first airline in the world to take delivery of the McDonnell Douglas MD-11, in November 1990.
Fleet: one McDonnell Douglas MD-11, two Airbus A300B4, five McDonnell Douglas DC-10-30, three McDonnell Douglas MD-87, five MD-82, five MD-83, 12 McDonnell Douglas DC-9-50, five DC-9-40; On order, three MD-82, three MD-11

Hapag-Lloyd Flug

This major German charter operator is a subsidiary of the Hapag Lloyd shipping line and was founded in 1972. In 1979 it absorbed Bavaria-German Air. The Hanover-based company flies holiday tours and charters to the Mediterranean, the Canaries, eastern Europe and West Africa.

Fleet: four Airbus A310-200, two A310-300; five Boeing 737-500, seven Boeing 737-400. On order one Airbus A310-300; five Boeing 737-500

Note: Two Boeing 737-200 and two Boeing 727-100 have been withdrawn from use and are for disposal.

Hawaiian Airlines

This airline was founded as Inter-Island Airways in 1929, operating Sikorsky amphibians between the islands. The present name was adopted in 1941. Today Hawaiian operates scheduled passenger services between the islands of Lanai, Maui, Molokai, Oahu, Kauai, Hilo and Kona. International services are flown to the South Pacific islands of American Samoa, Western Samoa, Tonga, Tahiti and Rarotonga, and also to Sydney. Flights are made to the continental US cities of Los Angeles, Las Vegas, San Francisco, Portland, Seattle and Anchorage. In early 1991 Northwest Airlines paid $20 million for a 25% holding in Hawaiian.

Fleet: six Lockheed L-1011-50; three McDonnell Douglas DC-8-72, three DC-8-62/63, one McDonnell Douglas DC-9-15F, twelve DC-9-51, one McDonnell Douglas MD-81; eight Boeing Canada Dash 7

Horizon Air

This Seattle-based airline was founded in 1981. In 1982 it swallowed Air Oregon and two years later Transwestern Airlines, making it the major regional airline for the northwest US. Scheduled passenger services are operated to 34 cities in the states of Washington, Oregon, Idaho, Montana and Utah. Since 1986 it has been a wholly owned subsidiary of Alaska Airlines. In mid 1991 Horizon signed an order for 35 (plus 25 options) Dornier 328s, the largest order so far placed for this new 30 seater commuter airliner. Deliverys will begin in 1993, gradually replacing the current Metro fleet.
Fleet: three Fokker F28-100; 15 Boeing Canada Dash 8-100; 32 Fairchild Metro III; On order, 35 Do.328, 5 DHC Dash 8-100.

Icelandair

Flugleidir RF

The original Icelandair was set up in 1937 and after World War II flew DC-3s, DC-4s and a Catalina amphibian to London, Glasgow and Oslo. Later it operated Viscounts.

The rival Icelandic Airlines was the operating name of Loftleidir, founded in 1944. It was famous for pioneering a low-fare transatlantic service in the 1950s and 1960s in DC-4s, and later in DC-6Bs, which staged through Reykjavik. The two airlines merged in 1973.

Today the airline operates domestic services over a ten-point network and scheduled international passenger services to European destinations. Icelandair ordered three Boeing 757-200s in May 1990 to replace its aging DC-8s.
Fleet: two Boeing 757-200, three Boeing 737-400; one Boeing 727-100C, five Fokker F.27-200; On order one Boeing 737-400, one Boeing 757-200; four Fokker 50.

Indian Airlines

With over 20,000 employees and carrying more than ten million passengers a year, Indian Airlines is one of the world's largest domestic carriers. It was formed in 1953, taking over the regional services of eight private operators. In the 1950s and 1960s, a fleet of DC-3s and Vickers Vikings, latterly supplemented by F27s and Viscounts, flew a huge network within the sub-continent itself and to Afghanistan, Burma, Nepal and Pakistan. Re-equipment with Airbuses began in 1986 but the airline suffered and services were disrupted by the crash of an A320 at Bangalore in early 1990. The airline operates scheduled passenger services to 73 cities including India's neighboring countries. As many as five A320s were used to assist in the evacuation of Indian nationals from the Persian Gulf area during 1990/91.
Fleet: 11 Airbus A300B4/B2, 18 Airbus A320; 24 Boeing 737-200, one 737-200C, three Fokker F27; On order, 12 Airbus A320

Intair

This major Canadian regional airline was formed in 1987 when Quebec Aviation, Quebecair and Nordair Metro merged. With operations centered on Montreal, Intair operates a network of scheduled passenger services across central and eastern Canada, with connections to Prince Edward Island and Newfoundland. Until 1989 the airline operated as a Canadian Partner in association with Canadian Airlines International, but since that date has traded as an independant airline.
Fleet: four Fairchild Metro (to be sold in 1991); seven Fokker F100

Iran Air

This carrier was formed in 1962 by the merger of the privately owned Iran Airways (usually known as Iranair) and Persian Air Services into a new state owned airline.

The merged airline initially grew rapidly but the 1979 Islamic revolution severely curtailed its growth and operational activities and a further setback occurred when one of its Airbus A300s was shot down in error by a US warship in 1988.

Scheduled passenger and freight services are flown to a variety of destinations and with improving international contacts, Iranair is looking at new routes. However problems still exist and the US government is currently blocking the sale of BAe.146s to Iranair.

Fleet: five Airbus A300B2, four Boeing 747SP, three Boeing 747-100/200, two 747F, four Boeing 707, four Boeing 727-200, two 727-100, three 737-200, six Fokker 100.

Japan Air System

This large Japanese domestic airline was formed in 1971 with the merger of Toa Airways and Japan Domestic Airlines. It operates a modern fleet along 66 routes to 38 cities throughout Japan.

Fleet: 16 Airbus A300B2/B4, one Airbus A300-600, two McDonnell Douglas DC-10-30ER, 19 McDonnell Douglas MD-81, four McDonnell Douglas MD-87, 12 McDonnell Douglas DC-9-40; 25 NAMC YS-11. On order, six Boeing 747-400, 12 Airbus A300-600; 13 McDonnell Douglas MD-81, six McDonnell Douglas MD-87, 10 McDonnell Douglas MD-90.

Japan Asia Airways

Formed in 1975 to operate services between Japan and Taiwan, this airline is a subsidiary of Japan Air Lines and operates scheduled passenger and cargo services from Tokyo and Osaka to Taipei and Hong Kong, and from the island of Okinawa to Taipei. Almost 1.4 million passengers were carried in 1990.

Fleet: three Boeing 747-100, one 747-200, one 747-300; four McDonnell Douglas DC-10-40

JAT

Jugoslovenski Aerotransport

The government-owned JAT was formed in 1947 to take control of all Yugoslav civil air transport activities. First-generation equipment included DC-3s, Junkers Ju 52/3ms and Ilyushin Il-14s, reflecting the nation's political stance between east and west. In the mid-1950s, JAT purchased three Convair CV340 and six Ilyushin Il-14P.

The airline operates an extensive domestic route network serving 16 destinations. Internationally flights are operated to 48 cities in Scandinavia, western and eastern Europe, the Middle and Far East, North America and Australia. Both charter and scheduled operations have been badly affected by the civil unrest in Yugoslavia during 1991.

Fleet: Three ATR72-200, 9 McDonnell Douglass DC-9-30, 4 McDonnell Douglass DC-10-30, eight Boeing 727-200, nine Boeing 737-300. On order; four McDonnell Douglas MD-11

Jersey European Airways

Formed in 1979, this small British independent has its headquarters at Exeter. Scheduled passenger services are flown to Belfast, Birmingham, Bournemouth, Exeter, the Isle of Man, London, Teeside and Southampton, and to Dinard and Paris. A major expansion was prepared for 1991, using six Fokker F27s leased from the Australian airline East West, and the airline hopes to establish a major presence at London (Stanstead) airport. The Bandierantes and Shorts 360s are currently leased to other operators and are available for sale.

Fleet: eight Fokker F27-500; three BAe.748, four Shorts 360; three Embraer Bandeirante.

Kenya Airways

The national carrier of Kenya was established in 1977 after the collapse of the East African Airways Corporation. Today the airline flies scheduled international passenger services to London, Paris, Rome, Athens, Frankfurt and Zurich, within Africa to Cairo, Khartoum, Addis Ababa, Mogadishu, Entebbe, Harare, Dar-es-Salaam, Lusaka, Kigali, Bujumbura, Ligongwe, Gaborone and Zanzibar, and also to Dubai and Jeddah. Domestic services are flown from Nairobi to Mombasa, Malindi and Kisumu.

Fleet: two Airbus A310-300; two Boeing 707-320B, one Boeing 720B (for sale), two Boeing 757; one McDonnell Douglas DC-8-73CF, one McDonnell Douglas DC-9-30; three Fokker F50, one Fokker F27-200.

Kuwait Airways

The Iraqi invasion of August 1990 forced Kuwait's national airline to operate temporarily from Cairo with its few remaining aircraft. Kuwait Airways returned home mid-1991 and have placed a massive order for Airbus aircraft to rebuild their fleet – deliveries due 1992.

The carrier had been formed as Kuwait National Airways Company in 1954 with two DC-3s, Viscounts later being acquired (1958). National was dropped from the title in 1957 and the following year BOAC took over technical management under a five-year contract. British International Airlines was taken over in 1959 and Trans Arabia Airways, flying DC-4s and -6s from Kuwait to Beirut, was taken over in 1964.

Fleet: (pre 1990) four Boeing 747-200 Combi, one Airbus A300C4-600, five Airbus A310-200, three Boeing 767-200ER, three Boeing 727-200, two Gulfstream III. On order 1991; 5 Airbus A300-600R, 3 A310-300, 3 A320, 4 A340-200 plus options.

Ladeco

This Chilean domestic airline was formed in 1958 as Línea Aérea del Cobre Ltda, with two DC-3s flying from Santiago to copper-mining centers in northern Chile. Today the airline, in which Ansett Transport Industries had a substantial holding, flies an extensive route network linking the capital with 16 destinations in this long, mountainous country. Regional services are flown to Mendoza in Argentina, Asunción, Guayaquil, Bogota, São Paulo and Rio de Janeiro. Flights are also made to Miami and New York and Washington.

Fleet: two BAC-111-300, three Boeing 707-320, four Boeing 727-100, two Boeing 737-200, one Boeing 737-300. On order; two Boeing 757-200.

LAM

LAM was founded in 1936 as DETA (Direcção de Exploração dos Transportes Aéreos), a division of the Railways and Airways administration of the former Portuguese East African colony. Its post-World War II equipment included two Junkers Ju-52/3m trimotors (which were kept flying into the 1960s), Lockheed Lodestars, DC-3s and DH Doves and Rapides. The company was renamed in 1980. Scheduled passenger services are flown from the capital, Maputo, to the port of Beira and to towns in the interior. Regional services are offered to Harare, Johannesburg and Dar-es-Salaam, and long-haul flights to Madrid, Lisbon, Paris, Copenhagen and Berlin.

Fleet: two Boeing 737-200, one Boeing 737-300, one McDonnell Douglas DC-10-30; one Ilyushin Il-62, two CASA C212, Two Beech King Air 200. On order; two Boeing 737-300, two Boeing 767-200ER.

LAN-Chile

Formed in 1929 as Línea Aeroposto Santiago-Arica or LASA, Chile's national airline acquired its present name in 1932 when it was taken over by the state. After World War II a small fleet of DC-3s, DC-6s and Martin 202s flew internal services, later reaching out to regional capitals and to Miami. In 1974 the carrier opened a route linking South America with Australia across the South Pole. Hit by recession at the end of 1990, the company announced its intention to sell off half its fleet, and cancelled orders for two Boeing 767s which would have been delivered in 1991.

Fleet: five Boeing 767-200ER, two Boeing 707-320, three Boeing 737-200; two BAe 146-200. On order three Boeing 767-200ER.

LAP

...nis, the national airline of Paraguay, was formed in 1962 and had ...trong links with the country's air force. Scheduled passenger services ...re flown to domestic destinations, to regional Latin American capitals ...nd to Miami, Madrid, Brussels and Frankfurt.

...leet: three Boeing 707-320B; one McDonnell Douglas DC-8-63, one ...C-8-61; one Lockheed L-188 Electra

Lauda Air

...ormed in 1979 by the champion Grand Prix racing driver Niki Lauda, ...his small Austrian airline operates holiday charter flights to the ...lediterranean and to Thailand and the Maldive Islands. Scheduled ...assenger services are operated from Vienna to Bangkok, Hong Kong ...nd Sydney. In 1991 the airline suffered a major tragedy with the loss ...f one of its almost new Boeing 767s over Thailand as a result of a ...hrust reverser malfunction.

...leet: two Boeing 767-300ER, one Boeing 737-400, two Boeing 737-...00. On order, one Boeing 767-300ER, two Boeing 737-400.

Liat

Based on the West Indian island of Antigua, Liat has a complex and commercially precarious history. It traces its origin to Leeward Islands Air Transport Services. This was set up in 1956 as a 51%-owned subsidiary of British West Indian Airways (BWIA), flying local services between Anguilla, Antigua, Barbados, Grenada and Trinidad with a couple of DH Herons and a Beech Twin Bonanza. The airline was sold in 1971 to the holiday company Court Line, which went bankrupt in 1974. The shares were bought by the local governments of Antigua, Barbuda, St Kitts and Nevis, Dominica, St Lucia, St Vincent and the Grenadines, Montserrat, Grenada, Barbados, Trinidad and Tobago, and Guyana.
Fleet: four BAe Super 748; seven Boeing Canada Dash 8-100; six DHC Twin Otter; two Pilatus Britten-Norman Islander

Linjeflyg

This company was set up in 1957 to operate domestic and charter services in Sweden. SAS held half the shares and newspaper publishers the rest. With five Convair 340/440s and eight DC-3s, night newspaper runs were an important part of the airline's early business. SAS sold their 50% holding to a Göteborg-based trucking company, while AB Aerotransport now own the rest (50%). Scheduled passenger services are operated across a 38-point domestic network and holiday charters are also undertaken. Linjeflyg has Europe's largest F28 fleet.
Fleet: five Boeing 737-500; one Boeing 737-300, three Fokker F28-1000, 16 F28-4000; eight Saab 340 (leased from Swedeair). On order ten Boeing 737-500

LOT

The Polish government formed Polski Linie Lotnicze in 1929 out of two private airlines, Aero TZ, and Aero LLoyd, both formed in 1922. It was an act of policy to provide a counter to the growing influence of Deutsche Lufthansa in central Europe. After World War II the shattered airline spluttered back into life with a handful of DC-3s and Lockheed 14s, later replaced by Soviet-supplied equipment including Lisunov Li-2s and Ilyushin Il-14s. Also, rather unusually, five French Languedocs were acquired in 1947. Ilyushin Il-18 turboprops and Il-62 jets followed in the 1960s. In 1988 the carrier ordered a fleet of Boeing 767-200ER aircraft for use on its long-distance routes. It thus became the first European airline to operate modern American jet equipment.

The airline operates domestic flights and international services to 36 countries.

Fleet: two Boeing 767-200ER; one Boeing 767-300ER, seven Ilyushin Il-62MK; eight Tupolev Tu 134A, thirteen Tu-154M, five Yak-40, three Ill-18, 8 Antonov An-24V, 2 An-26, one AN-12; On order, 8 ATR72.

Luxair

The national airline of the Duchy of Luxembourg was formed in 1961 as Luxembourg Airlines. It is 20%-owned by the government, the rest by banks and industrial holding companies. Scheduled passenger services are flown to Amsterdam, Copenhagen, Geneva, Athens, Faro, Frankfurt, Hamburg, Málaga, Palma, Paris, Rome, Nice and Munich. There are commuter and air taxi subsidiary companies.

Fleet: one Boeing 747SP, three Boeing 737-200; three Fokker 50; two Fokker F27-100. On order two Boeing 737-500, two Boeing 737-400; three Fokker 50, two EMB120 Brasilia.

Malev

The Hungarian state airline was formed in March 1946 as a joint Hungarian-Soviet venture (called Magyar-Szovjet Polgari Légiforgalani Tarsasag), using Lisunov Li-2s and Ilyushin Il-14s. In 1954 the Hungarian state acquired the Soviet 50% holding. Malev was one of the first eastern bloc countries to acquire western airliners. A BAe-146 QT was operated with TNT on an express parcels network which branched out to Budapest in 1990 in an venture which proved to be commercially unsuccessful. The airline flies scheduled passenger services to the capitals of Europe and to points in the Middle East and North Africa.
Fleet: three Boeing 737-200; three Boeing 737-200; one BAe 146-200QT; 142 Tupolev Tu-154B2, six Tupolev Tu134/134A; two Yakovlev Yak 40; On order, two Boeing 767-200ER.

Martinair

Founded in 1958 by J Martin Schröder, this diversified company has as the major part of its business, worldwide passenger and freight charters. The company has branched into inclusive tours and air taxi operations, with, in addition, an important in-flight service and catering subsidiary supplying other operators. Martinair maintains and operates under contract the Dutch government's VIP Fokker F28, and is the launch customer for the new convertible freighter version of the MD-11. Scheduled passenger and freight services are flown from Amsterdam to Baltimore, Detroit, Los Angeles, Miami, San Francisco, Minneapolis, New York, Seattle and Toronto.
Fleet: one Airbus A310-203, one A310-203C; two Boeing 747-200C, two Boeing 767-300ER; three McDonnell Douglas DC-10-30CF, one McDonnell Douglas MD-82; two Cessna Citation II, one Cessna 404 Titan. On order four Boeing 767-300ER

Mexicana

This was founded in 1921, making it the second oldest airline in the Americas. At one time it was wholly owned by Pan American who reduced their stake in the 1950s when the fleet was nearly all Douglas DC types: -3s, -4s and -6s. The first jets were three DH Comet 4Cs, ordered in 1960. In 1989 the Mexican government sold its remaining 54% shareholding to private investors. In 1990 the airline ordered a large number of Airbus A320s, with a strategy of competing head-on with the US mega-carriers. The first four were to be delivered during 1991. Today the airline operates from its Mexico City base to 30 points within the country. Connections are offered to all the major cities of the US, plus Havana, San Juan, Guatemala City, and San José in Costa Rica.
Fleet: 42 Boeing 727-200, five DC-10-15. On order 22 Airbus A320

Middle East Airlines

Throughout the travails of the civil war, Lebanon's Middle East Airlines has managed to keep flying, although services have been severely curtailed. MEA was formed by private business interests in 1945. It was assisted by Pan American from 1949 to 1955 when it became an associate of BOAC which took a 49% stake. In 1965 the company took over Air Liban which had grown with the help of Air France. In 1969 MEA also took over the Sabena protégé, Lebanese International Airways, which had operated from Beirut to points in the Middle East and to European capitals. Today the airline, conditions permitting, operates a network of scheduled passenger services in Europe, the Middle East and northwest Africa. In 1991 the airline was able to recommence operations from war torn Beiruit as fighting in the Lebanon subsided.
Fleet: three Boeing 747-200M, eight Boeing 707-320C, four Boeing 720B

Midway Airlines

This major US domestic regional operator began revenue-earning services in 1979. Air Florida was taken over in 1984. With hubs at Chicago and Philadelphia (opened in 1989), the airline flies scheduled passenger services to 54 destinations in the eastern and southeastern US. There are two commuter subsidiaries, Iowa Airways and Midway Commuter, jointly marketed under the banner of the Midway Connection. Midway sold its Philadelphia hub operation to USAir at the end of 1990 in a $65 million deal, and was forced to file for Chapter 11 protection in 1991 as the Gulf War and recession affected cash flow.
Fleet: 7 Boeing 737-200; nine McDonnell Douglas DC-9-15, 34 DC-9-30, four McDonnell Douglas MD-82, eight McDonnell Douglas MD-87, two MD-88, three MD-83, 12 EMB-120 Brasilia (leased from DLT), 21 Dornier Do 228. On order 33 Dornier Do 328 (Midway Connection); 25 McDonnell Douglas MD-82.

Midwest Express

This Milwaukee-based US regional airline was founded in 1984. From the hub it operates its 13-strong fleet to major US cities including Boston, Denver, Detroit, New York, Dallas/Fort Worth, Atlanta, Philadelphia, Kansas City, Los Angeles, San Francisco, San Diego, Washington DC, Fort Lauderdale and Tampa.
Fleet: eight McDonnell Douglas DC-9-10, three DC-9-30, two MD-88

Monarch

A major British holiday and charter airline carrying almost 3 million passengers a year, Monarch began operations in 1968 with Bristol Britanias. Today the airline has a fleet of Boeings and Airbuses, offering inclusive tour and seat-only flights to many Mediterranean resort destinations. The airline began operations to Miami in 1988, and to New York and Boston in 1990. Scheduled passenger services are flown to Mahon, Málaga and Tenerife. In addition to the aircraft listed below it also leases two Airbus A300s to Compass Airlines in Australia and operates a fleet of eight Boeing 737-300 on behalf of EuroBerlin. It also planned to purchase two Boeing 767s to be leased to fledgling Taiwan airline EVA, but these have subsequently been sold direct to EVA.

Fleet: two Airbus A300-600R; three Boeing 737-300; nine Boeing 737-200; nine Boeing 757-200. On order two Airbus A300-600R

Nationair

This Montreal-based Canadian charter airline began operations in 1984. Two years later it bought Quebecair's charter operations and its fleet of McDonnell Douglas DC-8s. Passenger and cargo charters are flown to Europe and South America and a scheduled passenger service from Montreal to Brussels. Following the bankruptcy of Soundair in 1990, Nationair acquired Odyssey to become Canada's third largest carrier.

Fleet: four Boeing 747-100/200, two Boeing 757; Four McDonnell Douglas DC-8-61, two DC-8-62, two DC-8-63

Note: one of the DC8s was lost following a crash during charter operations, Saudia Arabia, July 1991.

Nigeria Airways

The flag carrier of Nigeria traces its origin to West African Airways Corporation formed in 1946 to operate within the British colonies of Nigeria and the Gold Coast. When Ghana became independent in 1958 and withdrew from WAAC it was re-formed as Nigeria Airways in which BOAC held a 17% interest. Operations began with DC-3s flying domestic routes, while Britannias chartered from BOAC flew the Lagos-London route.

Today the airline offers scheduled passenger services over a comprehensive domestic route network within Nigeria, regional services to destinations in West and East Africa, and international services.
Fleet: four Airbus A310-200; two DC-10-30, two Boeing 707-320, eight Boeing 737-200; on order, one McDonnell Douglas MD-11
Note: several aircraft are not airworthy and are stored pending repairs.

PIA

Pakistan International Airway

Founded in 1954, it became a corporation a year later when it was merged with the smaller Orient Airways (founded in 1946). First-generation equipment included DC-3s operating services within West Pakistan and between West and East Pakistan (now Bangladesh). Lockheed Super Constellations flew long-haul routes and a Boeing 707 was acquired in 1960. Vickers Viscounts and Fokker F27 turboprops were operated from the late 1950s.

Today PIA flies to 32 domestic destinations, and offers scheduled passenger services to 40 points in 37 countries. The first of three A310s was delivered in June 1991.
Fleet: six Boeing 747-200B, two 747-200 Combi, eight Airbus A300B4, one Airbus A310-300, six Boeing 737-300, four 707-320C, one 707-320B, fourteen Fokker F.27-200, two DHC Twin Otter; On order, two Airbus A310-300.

Royal Jordanian Airlines

Formerly known as Alia, the national carrier of Jordan was founded in 1963. In early 1990 the airline agreed a $40 million leasing deal for 12 years on six Airbus A320s but suffered a big downturn in operating revenue after the Iraqi invasion of Kuwait.

When war actually broke out in January 1991 the airline adopted a temporary hub at Vienna for long-haul operations but in the Middle East itself the carrier was forced to reduce operations from Amman to a bare minimum – flying to Larnaca, Cairo and Vienna only.

Before the crisis scheduled passenger and cargo services were flown from the capital, Amman, to destinations all over the Middle East, the Gulf and northwest Africa.

Fleet: Three Airbus A320, six Airbus A310-300, three Boeing 727-200, three Boeing 707-320, five Lockheed L-1011 Tristar 500; On order, five Airbus A320, five Airbus A340-200/300.

SkyWest

Utah-based SkyWest is a US commuter airline, formed in 1972. Operating under the Delta Express marketing banner, it feeds Delta Airline's hubs at Los Angeles and Salt Lake City. SkyWest's twin-prop fleet brings in passengers from 42 cities in the mid-west and west of the US. In 1991 it controversially cancelled its options on the Canadair RJ and instead placed extra orders for the fast turboprop Saab 2000. Currently it has the distinction of being the leading operator at Los Angeles International Airport in terms of aircraft movements although, tragically, one of its Metros was lost in a collision on the runway during early 1991.

Fleet: eleven Embraer EMB-120 Brasilia; 37 Fairchild Metro. On order 20 Saab 2000; seven Embraer EMB-120 Brasilia

Southwest Air Lines

SWAL was formed in 1967 to operate a service in the Ryukyu islands, the 300-mile chain stretching southwest from the Japanese home island of Kyushu to Okinawa. Previously the services had been operated by Air America. The airline is based on Okinawa and scheduled passenger services link Naha airport with most of the islands in the Ryukyus and the Sakishima Shoto groups.
Fleet: eight Boeing 737-200; five NAMC YS-11A; four DHC Twin Otter: On order, four Boeing 737-400.

Southwest Airlines

This Dallas-based airline ranks 38th in the world in terms of annual sales. It was formed in 1967 as Air Southwest to service a growing market for low-fare air travel within Texas. The present name was adopted in 1971. Today the airline flies its large fleet of Boeing 737-200s and -300s to 31 US airports in 14 states.
Fleet: 50 Boeing 737-300, 46 737-200, ten 737-500. On order 12 Boeing 737-300, 38 737-500.

Syrianair

The state airline of Syria was restructured in 1961 to succeed Syrian Airways, which had itself been founded in 1946. Following the short-lived union of Egypt and Syria in 1960-61, the two countries had formed United Arab Airlines with an ambitiously modern fleet of Comets and Viscounts. Syrian Arab Airlines, to give it its full title, flies from Damascus to Aleppo, Latakia and Deirezzor, and to major cities in Europe, North Africa, the Middle and Far East.

The current fleet is a mixed collection of Soviet and western airliners, including two Caravelles. Syria's co-operation with the western allies in the Gulf War may provide the opportunity to modernise the fleet.

Fleet: three Boeing 727-200, two Boeing 747SP; two Caravelle 10B; two Dassault Falcon 20F; five Antonov An-26, one Antonov An-24; four Ilyushin Il-76; three Tupolev Tu-154M, six Tupolev Tu-134; six Yakovlev Yak-40

TAP

Transportes Aeroes Portugueses was founded in 1944 as a department of the ministry of transport and began operations flying from Lisbon to Casablanca with a Lockheed L18 Lodestar. Scheduled services began with a DC-3 in 1946. In 1953 the operation was acquired by private business and merged with Aero Portuguesa, founded in 1934. It was built up to serve Portugal's African and Asian colonies and points in Europe with a fleet of Constellations and DC-6Bs. A route to London was flown jointly with BEA using the latter's Viscounts and Comet 4Bs. In 1962 TAP took delivery of its first jet, a Caravelle. TAP was nationalized following the revolution of 1975, the first Boeing 727s being delivered in that year.

Fleet: six Airbus A310-300; two Boeing 727-200, nine 737-200, one 737-200C, five 737-300; seven Lockheed L-1011 TriStar500; on order two Airbus A340

TAROM

The Romanian state airline began operating in 1954 with Soviet-supplied Li-2s and Ilyushin Il-14s. Its current equipment – a mix of eastern, western and home-built (Rombac One-Elevens) aircraft – reflects the former dictatorship's changing relationships with the European power blocs. In spite of post-revolution operating problems, Tarom maintain a network of internal passenger and cargo services, plus international scheduled passenger services to European capitals, to Tripoli, Algiers and Casablanca, Amman, Beirut, Cairo, Damascus, Istanbul, Abu Dhabi, Larnaca and Tel Aviv, Karachi, Bangkok, Singapore, Beijing and New York.

Fleet: four Boeing 707-320C; seven BAe One-Eleven-500, three One-Eleven 400; six Rombac One-Eleven-500; 27 Antonov An-24RV, 7 Antonov An-26; five Ilyushin Il-62/62M, 9 Ilyushin Il -18; 10 Tupolev Tu-154B. On order three Airbus A310-300.

TAT

This French airline was formed in 1968 as Touraine Air Transport and grew gradually from air-taxi operator to major regional carrier by taking over other competitors, including Air Paris, Rousseau Aviation, Air Alpes and Air Alsace. An extensive network of scheduled passenger services is operated from Paris (Orly) and from Lyons. A seasonal summer service is flown from Tours and Poitiers in midwestern France to London (Gatwick). In addition, TAT flies a number of services on behalf of Air France.

Fleet: five Boeing 737-200, four Fokker 100, 12 Fokker F28-1000, four F28-2000, five F28-4000, one Fokker 100; 8 Fairchild FH-227B, two Fairchild F27A, three Fairchild Metro; eight ATR 42-300; three DHC Twin Otter; four Beech 99. On order four ATR 42, 14 ATR 72; 12 Fokker 100.

THY-Turkish Airlines

he present operation was formed in 1956 as a joint state and privately
wned enterprise flying a largely domestic network with a fleet of DC-3s
nd DH Herons. The first turboprop equipment consisted of Fokker
27s and Vickers Viscounts, operating local links and international
ights to Nicosia and Rome. Today THY is wholly state-owned, operat-
g a network of internal scheduled passenger services linking the
najor centers of Ankara, Istanbul, Antalya, Izmir and Adana with 11
ther domestic destinations. International scheduled services are
own to Europe, the Middle East, North Africa and the US. Kibris Türk
lava Yollari, the airline of northern Cyprus, is a subsidiary.
leet: seven Airbus A310-200, six A310-300; two Boeing 707-320,
ine Boeing 727-200, two 737-400; nine McDonnell Douglas DC-9-30.
)n order one Airbus A310-300, five Airbus A340; eight Boeing 737-
00 (to be leased), three BAe ATP.

TNT

he air freight arm of the Australian-controlled TNT transport group
egan operations in 1968. In 1984 came a move into Europe with the
stablishment of an operating hub in Cologne with several sub-centers.
he workhorse of the operation is a fleet of BAE 146-200QT (Quiet
rader) optimized for flying overnight parcel services from city to city.
oint ventures at the outset of the 1990s with the Hungarian airline
Malev and Aeroflot have proved commercially disappointing but other
perations including those in Spain, Sweden and Italy, as well as the
nited Kingdom, are working well. XP Express is a subsidiary operat-
g division.
leet: 11 BAe 146-200QT six BAe 146-300QT; one Fokker F27-600F.
)n order four BAe 146-300QT

Trans European Airways

This Belgian-based charter operator was founded in 1970. It operates holiday charter and inclusive tour flights to Mediterranean and other resort destinations with a fleet of Airbus and Boeing 737s. Subsidiaries include TEA-UK, the former Mediterranean Express, operating inclusive tour charters from Birmingham and Newcastle to Spain, Greece, Portugal, Italy and Tunisia. Other subsidiaries are based in France and Switzerland.

Fleet: 2 Airbus A310-300, 25 Boeing 737-300. On order, 10 Airbus A310-300; 17 Boeing 737-300/400.

Note: Fleet list includes all subsiduaries.

Varig

Viacão Aérea Rio de Janeiro-Grandens

This privately owned Brazilian airline is the country's oldest. Dornier Wal flying boats were used by the fledgling airline to fly routes north and south along the coast from Rio, starting in 1927.

It absorbed the domestic airline, Aéro Geral, in 1951, the REAL consortium with its huge fleet of DC-3s and DC-6s in 1961 and in 1965 Panair do Brasil, in which Pan Am then held a 30% interest.

Today Varig operates an extensive series of routes throughout South and Central America, and to the US, Europe and Japan.

Fleet: three Boeing 747-200B Combi, two 747-300 Combi, three 747-300, six 767-200ER, 4 Boeing 767-300ER, six 727-100, four 727-100C, 11 737-200, 15 737-300, two McDonnell-Douglas DC-10-30F, ten DC-10-3, five Boeing 707-320C, two Airbus A300B4, 14 Lockheed L-188 Electra; on order six MD-11, 21 Boeing 737-300, 2 Boeing 767-300ER, eight McDonnell Douglass MD-11, eight Boeing 747-400.

VIASA

The national carrier of Venezuela was created in 1961, largely out of the existing international services of Avensa and LAV (Línea Aeropostal Venezuelana), inheriting their existing long-haul fleet, including six Lockheed L-1049 Super Constellations and two Douglas DC-6Bs. The first jet equipment included DC-8s and Convair 880s. Today the airline operates Airbus A300s and DC-10s from Caracas, Maracaibo, Porlamar and Barcelona to major European capitals, the US and major Caribbean and Latin American cities. In 1989 the airline began a service to Havana.

Fleet: three Airbus A300B4; six McDonnell Douglas DC-10-30. On order two McDonnell Douglas MD-11

Virgin Atlantic

Formed by the entrepreneur Richard Branson in 1984 with a single Boeing 747, the airline has grown slowly but steadily into a major long haul operator. It currently flies from London to Miami, Los Angeles, New York, Moscow and Tokyo while charter flights are operated regularly to Orlando.

As Virgin has matured, its image has slowly evolved from that of a cut price transatlantic carrier to one that offers solid competition to the business traveller.

After a fierce legal battle, and bitter opposition from British Airways, Virgin Atlantic was permitted to begin operations from London Heathrow. In addition it was also permitted to take over some of British Airways landing slots at Tokyo's crowded Narita Airport, allowing two additional weekly round trips.

Fleet: One Boeing 747-100, seven Boeing 747-200.

Yemenia

This was formed in 1963 as Yemen Airlines, the national airline of the Yemen Arab Republic. The present name was adopted in 1978 when the airline was reorganized, with the Yemeni government and Saudi Arabia holding respectively 51% and 49% of the capital. In 1990 the airlines of North and South Yemen, Alyemda and Yemenia, agreed to merge. A network of domestic routes is operated from the operating base at Sana'a – with international scheduled passenger services to cities including Amman, Doha, Jeddah, Sharjah, Khartoum, Addis Ababa, Karachi, Damascus, Riyadh, Cairo, Rome, London, Amsterdam, Istanbul, Moscow, Frankfurt, Bombay, and Paris.
Fleet: (Yemenia) six Boeing 727-200, two Boeing Canada Dash 7. (Alyemda – Democratic Yemen Airlines) two Boeing 707-320C, two Boeing 737-200C; two Boeing Canada Dash 7; one Tupolev 154

Zambia Airways

The national carrier of Zambia was formed in 1967, soon after independence, with initial technical support from Alitalia and then from Aer Lingus. A small fleet operates scheduled passenger and freight services to points within Zambia from the capital, Lusaka. International services are flown to Nairobi, Dar-es-Salaam, Harare, Gaborone, Johannesburg, Jeddah, Entebbe, Frankfurt, London, Rome, New York and Bombay.
Fleet: One Boeing 757PF, two Boeing 737-200; two ATR 42-300; one McDonnell Douglas DC-8-71, one McDonnell Douglas DC-10-30.

INDEX

Acknowledgements

All *color artwork profiles* copyright © Greenborough Associates, except for the following: Mike Badrocke p16 (bottom), p.26 (top), p.23 (bottom).
All *color photographs* in this book by Mark Wagner, except for the following: All Nippon Airlines p.47; David Cooper p.38; Mike Jerram p.42, p.84, p.112, p.124, p.136, p.148, p.149; Korean Air p.76; Leo Marriott p.71, p.113 (top), p.123 (bottom), p.127 (top), p.155 (bottom); US Air p.110.
All *black and white photographs* by Christy Campbell.

Book design: Hussain R. Mohamed.